the Spiritual Legacy
of **Shaolin Temple**

the
Spiritual
Legacy *of*
Shaolin
Temple

Buddhism, Daoism, and the Energetic Arts

BY ANDY JAMES

Wisdom Publications • Boston

Wisdom Publications
199 Elm Street
Somerville, MA 02144 USA
www.wisdompubs.org

Library of Congress Cataloging-in-Publication Data

James, Andy.
  The spiritual legacy of Shaolin temple : Buddhism, Daoism, and the energetic arts / by Andy James.
     p. cm.
  Includes bibliographical references.
  ISBN 0-86171-352-4 (pbk. : alk. paper)
  1. Qi gong. 2. Zen Buddhism and Martial arts—China. 3. Shao lin si (Dengfeng Xian, China) I. Title.
  RA781.8.J36 2004
  613.7'148—dc22
                              2004015424

First Edition
09 08 07 06 05 04
6   5   4   3   2   1

Wisdom Publications' books are printed on acid-free paper and meet the guidelines for the permanence and durability set by the Council of Library Resources.

Cover design by Katya Popova
Interior design by Potter Publishing. Set in Acaslon 10.5/12.

Cover photograph: "West Peak of Hua-Shan, Shensi Province" [detail], by Steven R. Johnson. Reprinted with permission from Where the World Does Not Follow: Buddhist China in Picture and Poem. All rights reserved.

Printed in Canada

Contents

Foreword

Across the span of ancient Chinese history, families and tribes cultivated martial arts skills and developed them into a variety of unique combative systems. Through years of intense combat, these systems were eventually refined into an amazing art of deadly functionality. Because knowledge is power, the most esoteric aspects of each combat system were kept hidden, for secrecy always gave one an advantage over potential assailants.

The ancient Chinese martial, medical, and spiritual skills have long been influenced by the various stories and accounts of warrior kings, Daoist shaman mystics, and Buddhist immortals with magical powers. Such stories enhanced the influence and prestige of martial, medical, and spiritual systems.

In this book Shifu Andy James gives us the true history and evolution of the Shaolin, Daoist, and Chan (Zen) Buddhist systems and disposes of the misconceptions and widespread cultural distortions surrounding these disciplines. James's in-depth understanding of Chinese integral mind-body training stems from his thirty-five years of personal internal martial arts experience. Included are invaluable accounts of energetic and spiritual transformations and priceless insights that he has garnered from over twenty years as an internal martial arts and meditation instructor.

A master instructor internationally recognized by his peers for his mastery of the most esoteric aspects of the internal martial arts, Shifu Andy James is eminently qualified to present this information to the public, and I am very pleased to be introducing him and this book to you.

Jerry Alan Johnson
Executive Director of the International Institute of Medical Qigong

Preface

Thanks to thousands of martial arts movies, TV shows, comedy skits, and the like, Buddha statues, yin-yang symbols, and shaven-headed fighting monks are now part of popular culture. For over thirty years I have had an insider's view of this popularizing trend, initially as a student and then as a teacher. For most of this period, I assumed that the widening media exposure would lead to a steadily increasing number of students of Eastern traditions and this in turn would benefit society. But now I find myself saddened by what I currently see in the media (much of which is inaccurate and at times insulting) and by the many people I meet who feel they have the measure of these traditions because they have seen some movies, read a few books, surfed the Internet, or maybe taken a weekend workshop or a few classes…in short, tried the flavor of the month.

I am concerned about this trend, not because I want more students or more acclaim for my particular practices, but because we live in critical times and we urgently need personal and collective transformation. I sense that the Western search for enlightenment that began in the 1960s and 1970s sometimes seems to have been sidetracked in more recent decades. We seem to be hurtling toward a dubious sci-fi future, and many fear the opportunities for changing our direction are rapidly diminishing.

In this context, I feel that Buddhism, Daoism, and the martial arts deserve deeper inquiry and consideration—but before I explain why, I want to point out that the cultural distortion and trivialization these disciplines have suffered are not isolated occurrences but part of a widespread phenomenon. One of the biggest misconceptions we hold about the

Information Age is that information by itself somehow makes us wiser. The futurist John Naisbitt warns that "the most dangerous promise of technology is that it will make our children smarter.... Access to information will not teach synthesis and analysis. School expenditures on information technology reached $4.34 billion in 1997, yet at the same time programs for music and the arts were defunded."[1] There is mounting evidence that many of us are already suffering from information overload. Overwhelmed by too much information and complexity, we numb ourselves and turn off our attention almost entirely.

In terms of spiritual transformation, the limits of mere information and of the thinking process are even more pronounced. The ego is just one of the levels of consciousness. For true mind-body health, all levels need to be in balance. Although we may read about different enlightenment traditions or may have had an extraordinary experience, this by no means automatically and permanently elevates our consciousness. Traditional spiritual teaching suggests that higher realization requires persistent and skillful practice, usually under the guidance of an experienced teacher. Many of us tend to think that our consciousness is more evolved than it actually is. We talk the talk but do not match it with the walk.

The communications revolution has created not only more information but also an immensely powerful mass media machine, bolstered by new technologies and corporate concentration. This has happened so quickly that its power is hard to estimate. We may feel that we are mature enough not to be affected by what we see on the screen or hear because it is not "real" the way a physical blow or the theft of property is real. Truly, though, this is an absurd (and dangerous) denial, since the entertainment-advertising-media industry is one of the most successful and the fastest growing, targeting our children even before they can walk. It is skilled in shaping our opinions and tastes, and is a powerful tool, not only of giant corporations but also of our own government.

Our everyday lives are beginning to overlap with the screen world and are even being shaped by it. North American TV stations invariably show *Ben Hur* and *The Ten Commandments* every Easter as if they were documentaries or ersatz church services. Witness Mel Gibson's *The Passion of the Christ*. It's arguable many murders, massacres, and rapes have been patterned after elements in the media. When the twin towers of the World Trade Center came tumbling down on September 11, 2001, the event had an eerie sense of sci-fi and disaster movie déjà vu, replete with frantic hordes running along concrete canyons, chased by billowing clouds of smoke and debris. The media and political leaders spun predictably simplistic and heart-rending stories of heroes and villains, just like a Hollywood movie script or a glorified reality TV show. Though we are seeing more now, initially there was less real soul-searching or inquiry than we might hope—questioning whether we had somehow brought this on. We lost a precious opportunity to explore complex but urgent matters like the clash of cultures and religions, the American-dominated "globalization," or the widening gap between rich and poor.

One may reasonably ask, what possible relevance could a 1,500-year-old tradition of fighting monks have to our current, technology-driven lives, apart from being grist for mindless entertainment?

We can start by considering a remarkable historical fact—the small, obscure Shaolin Temple in Henan Province, China, was the birthplace not only of one of the most famous branches of Buddhism (Chan, perhaps more familiar in its Japanese transliteration, Zen) but also of a martial arts lineage that over the centuries has influenced the combat systems of China and then Japan, Korea, Thailand, the Philippines, and probably Indonesia as well. These martial systems influenced Asian military conflicts (and therefore politics) over the ages and in the last century have given rise to a variety of globally popular sports, mind-body fitness systems, and art forms.

Many books have been written on the comprehensive fighting techniques developed in the Shaolin Temple and many more on the history, evolution, and techniques of Zen Buddhism. It is difficult to find any, however, that explore Shaolin's unique combination of spiritual and martial arts training. Are these two parallel, independent developments or have they been creatively interconnected from the start? This book examines just that, inquiring into what factors produced a magnificent spiritual lineage and a superb martial lineage in the same remote temple.

It is evident that within the confines of the Shaolin Temple a unique elixir was created, a blend of lofty Indian metaphysics and the straightforward practicality of the Chinese mind and culture. It combined the genius of Buddhism and Daoism, both of which emphasize continual change and interdependence upon causes and conditions within our lives and our environment; in both of these systems, nothing is as solid and separate as it seems. The monks of Shaolin underwent a spiritual training that included meditation, rigorous physical and martial training, and breathing exercises designed to balance and enhance the subtle energies (*qi*, alternatively transliterated as *chi*, and also familiar in the Japanese transliteration, *ki*). This mind-body training embraced all aspects of human development and capability, encompassing the archetypal Warrior, Healer, and Sage.

Much of the wisdom of Shaolin resonates with the rhythms of our time. Our science is beginning to encounter what the monks of Shaolin have long known. We can see this in cutting-edge explanations of quantum physics. And after much resistance, modern medicine is finally admitting that the mind interacts with what we regarded as a purely physical body, and the boundaries between what is inside us and what is outside are no longer so obvious. Psychology is continuing to explore the possibilities of the transpersonal. The West is more curious about what the East has to offer, especially regarding spirituality and healing. A study published in the *New England Journal of Medicine* found that in 1990 out-of-pocket

expenditures on "unconventional therapy" in the United States amounted
to $10.3 billion, which was comparable to the $12.8 billion spent out-of-
pocket on hospitalization.

In developed Western countries, the grassroots movement toward
wholistic health is growing steadily despite criticism from conventional
hardheaded sources. For many people wholistic health simply means
natural foods and herbs. Others may venture into alternative medicine,
therapies, or yoga and Eastern martial arts. Others meld their spiritual
practices with shamanism, psychic or occult experience, or meditation.
Many wholistic or wellness centers now offer eclectic combinations of
such practices alongside conventional Western trainings—weightlifting,
aerobics, and the like. Many integrative systems are emerging. George
Leonard and Michael Murphy have used their extensive Esalen experience to develop an Integral Transformative Practice (ITP), which they
describe as a "long-term program for realizing the potential of body, mind,
heart, and soul." It includes affirmation, visualization, meditation, aikido,
yoga, aerobic exercise, and more.

It is not an easy task, however, to adapt ancient spiritual traditions
from foreign cultures into effective tools for modern living. On the one
hand, these traditions cannot simply be transplanted into the West with
all their redundant cultural bells and whistles; they need to be adapted.
On the other hand, if we are too extravagant in chopping up traditional
systems and reassembling the parts into eclectic, marketable systems, we
may lose the vital ingredient of wholism—the sense of being a whole.
More parts do not necessarily make a greater whole.

In this book I offer up my experiences and place them within a context of reflections on the integral mind-body training that began evolv-
ing in the Shaolin Temple and other parts of China well over a thousand
years ago. The traditions I draw upon have been time tested, refined,
and integrated, philosophically and practically, for many centuries. I feel
the broad legacy of Shaolin Temple is a valuable model for human de-

velopment. I hope my personal story and reflections may help illuminate this legacy.

I find the traditions precious and amazing in their intricate consistency and ageless wisdom, and I hope they will resonate with you as well.

Acknowledgments

I dedicate this book to the memory of Miss Rose Li, who passed away on July 29, 2001, in London, England. She was my first and main teacher of the internal martial arts—*taijiquan, xingyiquan,* and *baguazhang.* Ironically, although she shunned many traditional customs, she embodied the noblest aspects of a bygone age.

Robert Smith wrote of her in his book *Martial Musings:*

> The best female internal boxer I ever met (and that includes the exquisite Jasmine Dong of Hong Kong) was Rose Li…. She began boxing at age eight during the 1920s under the renowned Deng Yunfeng, a xingyi student of Geng Jishan and an associate of Sun Lutang, Shang Yunxiang, and other leading boxers…. Liu Fengshan (a.k.a. Liu Caizhen), a famous student of Yang Banhou's pupil, Wu Quanyu, came regularly to teach taiji to Rose and other interested students…. In Beijing in the 1930s, she recalled, it was not customary for boxers to distinguish different schools of taiji from each other, for instance Yang Style, Wu style and so on. Rather, it was generally accepted that each master assimilated the traditional teachings and adapted them to his own needs and physique…. Her view is that the "internal" refers to the internal self and is used to distinguish boxing for self-cultivation from boxing for display. External boxing is impressive, flamboyant, often very acrobatic, and always practiced for an external purpose—sport, self-defense, or demonstration.

I would like to acknowledge my other longtime teacher, Dhiravamsa, who trained me as a vipassana teacher and encouraged me to teach. What he taught me is always in my heart, and meditation has long been the foundation of everything I do. I am also deeply grateful to Dr. Jerry Alan Johnson, who has generously instructed me over the years in the many aspects of qigong and also in baguazhang. His practical knowledge of the internal arts is encyclopedic.

I am grateful to the following masters for sharing their respective arts with me and my students: the gifted Chungjen Chang of Taiwan, who now resides in Maryland; the renowned Wudang, Shaolin, and Xingyiquan master Professor Liu Yuzeng of Zhengzhou, China. I am also grateful to master Zhang Yufei of Beijing, who instructed me in Hunyuan Chen style taijiquan.

I would like to express my deep appreciation to my longtime students for their continuing support and especially to the following for their on-going contribution as teachers: Donna Oliver, Sheila Furness, Jeff Willis, Colin Outram, Suzanne Takahashi, Anna Strzelecka, and Ken Poole. I am grateful to Bob Youngs for his support in the past.

I always derive great love, comfort, and support from my family: my daughters Shuwen, Shuwei, and Hana, my partner Nicola, my mother Beryl, and my brothers, Brian, Michael, and Ray.

Section I: Introduction

1

The Author's Story

A Sunny Childhood

I was not raised in the tradition of Buddhism or Daoism, nor was I brought up with the martial arts. They came to me as if by accident. Although of Chinese descent, I was born in the tiny South American country of Guyana (though it was then known as British Guiana), where the population is predominantly East Indian and black, the language is English, and the main religion is Christianity. Culturally, we felt kinship with the British West Indies (especially Trinidad, Barbados, and Jamaica), Britain, and the United States. My early childhood was sunny and calypso-carefree, playing soccer and cricket and riding my bike all over town. I loved movies, especially Westerns.

Although our family was Church of England, my parents sent me to a large Roman Catholic primary school for academic reasons. The pupils there were from all social strata, and playground fights abounded. The teachers, including some nuns, liberally used the cane on hands and bottoms. For one nun who taught first grade, the preferred punishment was locking children in small cupboards. I can attest that the experience was not only claustrophobic but extremely hot.

While a schoolboy I somehow came up with the idea to use what would now be called affirmation and visualization to curb my explosive temper and to overcome my fear of certain teachers and playground bullies. I remember picturing a particularly fierce teacher and repeating to myself over and over, "He is only a human being, just like me." These self-taught techniques worked well for me. I had not shared my fears and concerns with anyone because I felt I was expected to be tough. At about the age of seven, I became fascinated with the Roman Catholic rituals and voluntarily prayed at the Stations of the Cross at least once a day, catching the approving attention of the local Jesuit priest. When I was ten, I won a national scholarship to the secondary school of my choice.

In 1962, I was forced to grow up in a hurry. Just short of my thirteenth birthday, a general strike erupted into violent riots. As looters swarmed around my father's business premises, someone thrust a machete into my hands and told me to keep the looters at bay, but fortunately some of the looters thought my father was a good person and persuaded the mob to move on. Riots swirled, buildings burned, and people were beaten and killed all day. Late that night, my elder brother and I, ignorant of the curfew, were nearly shot by British soldiers who had just landed. Somehow, while riding in my brother's car, we both heard and recognized the urgent metallic cocking of a machine gun and screeched to a halt.

Culture Shock

My family was so shocked and traumatized by the violence that erupted among what had hitherto been a gentle and good-natured people that, a few weeks later, we moved to London. I had never even thought about England and was unprepared for the damp cold of March, the gray skies, the smog, and the grimy brick buildings. Life seemed cold and hard-edged in comparison to the land of my birth. Having to wear heavy clothing and to stay indoors so much, I contracted. For the first time, I also felt self-conscious. I looked different (Chinese) and sounded different (West Indian), and was now living in the most accent-conscious country in the world.

My self-consciousness and sense of isolation increased when my parents enrolled me in an English public school, which, contrary to what the name implies, is actually a privileged, private boarding school. Public schools are noted for their old-fashioned customs, which are supposed to toughen pupils and turn them into well-rounded and educated English gentlemen. In my school of several hundred students, I could easily count the nonwhite faces on the fingers of my two hands. I felt very alone—especially since I had never spent even a few days away from my family.

It was fortunate for me that at thirteen or fourteen I was relatively big for my age (almost my present size), because bullying was an accepted practice at English public schools. Unlike at day schools, at a boarding school you cannot run home after classes and therefore have to be always on guard. Anyone who was not "normal" was targeted for cruel treatment by many of the other students. The ones I ended up spending my time with were the other oddballs—those who were thin, fat, short, tall, goofy looking, non-English, or lower-class. We banded together to help each other but tended to fall victim to the band of bullies one by one. When my turn eventually came around, I warned the ringleader that they had better beat me up real good because he was going to be my first lead-pipe victim when I recovered. They passed me over that time, but I was targeted in subtler ways by the prefects (older student officials). This was more hurtful than the outright bullies since they were supposed to be mature and held positions of trust and authority.

Apart from the bullying by the students and occasional caning from the teachers, I adapted to English school life and did well in both sports and academic work. I took the cultural changes of the "Swinging Sixties" easily in stride because everything was new to me anyway. I frequented discotheques and pubs, and partied with my brother Brian (who was five years older) and his friends. Despite this, I became increasingly introspective and read a lot during my spare time at school. I liked works on psychology and poetry and started writing my own poems. By the end of secondary school I had become somewhat socialist and antireligious, agreeing with Marx that in most cases religion functions as "the opium of the people."

I was accepted into the notorious London School of Economics (LSE), which was the training ground of many who would go on to be Third World leaders and political radicals. The Rolling Stones' Mick Jagger gave up his studies there just before I started. In spite of my radical rhetoric, I saw myself as still ruled by down-to-earth common sense and followed my father's prodding to enter the business stream, taking economics and specializing in accounting and finance.

Wake-Up Calls

I started at LSE in 1967, just as the sixties were turning nasty. The anti-war and student protest movements were picking up steam. Demonstrations and debates were common at LSE, a center of the protest movement. These discussions often spilled over into private parties and, I dimly recall, drunken all-night political arguments. During a visit to Guyana, I even argued ideals with the man who would soon become the socialist president of Guyana, Forbes Burnham, during one of my parents' social gatherings.

In the summer of 1968, at the age of nineteen, I received one of life's wake-up calls. While on a tour of Scandinavia I was chatting with an African student and his attractive Finnish companion at a Helsinki student hostel when a hefty, muscular off-duty Finnish soldier came over to our table and sat down. Quite drunk, he started insulting my new acquaintance and asked the young woman why she went out with foreigners like this "black monkey." After unsuccessfully trying to pacify him, we left for our rooms—but the soldier followed, eventually pushing and slapping my friend. I was smaller than the soldier, but my African friend was positively tiny. Before I could think about what I was doing, I grabbed the soldier by the shoulder and pushed him away, yelling at him to stop.

He went into a rage, bellowed, and threw a few punches, which to my surprise I managed to dodge. He then charged like a bull. I considered the situation in seeming slow motion and concluded my only opportunity to escape serious injury was an ungentlemanly kick to his groin. In a split second, I had kicked him with all my might, almost lifting him from the ground. He did not fall and scream in agony as I had pictured, but he did immediately become, as it were, amenable to reason and soon departed.

I don't think I was traumatized by this encounter, but it did give me pause. Some people are unreasonably violent, and sometimes the spur to violence is racism. Being nonwhite and smaller than the average European, I figured that the probability of my being a target of such violence was higher than average. Reviewing the technical side of my Finnish Encounter, I noted that speed can overcome superior strength and size.

A few months later, on my way to classes at LSE, a karate poster in the London subway caught my eye, and after watching a class I impulsively enrolled for lessons in both karate and judo. The *sensei* (teacher) was a jovial Belgian named George Mayo, who asked us to address him as "Chief." He said that his style, Kyushindo, was softer and more flowing than better-known Japanese styles like Shotokan. He made mysterious references to the Chinese martial arts, which he said were the original forms, and were more sophisticated than the Japanese-derived ones. I felt excited at discovering this whole new world, but at the same time somewhat foolish. After all, I was of Chinese descent but knew nothing of Chinese language, philosophy, history, or martial arts. And I was learning Japanese-style karate from a Belgian!

My initial experience of karate was exhilarating. I got to wear an exotic white uniform and could use my whole body—punching, chopping, leaping, and kicking. Sparring (fighting with only light contact) with fellow students was much more primal and honestly competitive than any other sport (even rugby and boxing) that I had tried, yet the goal was not to hurt or injure. I found again that I could compensate for my smaller size with agility, speed, intelligence, and spirit; I could maximize the efficacy of my body-mind package in a unique and liberating fashion. The martial arts touched something deep within me, and I made a commitment to practice daily and to excel. This kind of total commitment was new for me, although I was always good in academics and sports. Before this, nothing had inspired me to commit fully to it, since nothing seemed to be worth the effort.

I began reading about the history and theory of martial arts and quickly gravitated to the Chinese martial arts, popularly known at that time as *kung fu.* I discovered that these were much older and more varied than the better-known (in the West) systems like Japanese karate and Korean *taekwondo.* I started going to all the kung-fu movies I could find in Chinatown, since genuine teachers of the Chinese martial arts were relatively rare in London at that time. Even kung fu movies were unknown in mainstream cinemas.

Intrigued by what other treasures the East might have to offer, I bought a book on the Indian hatha yoga and began practicing on my own. For the first time, I started reading about the body's vital energies (called in yoga *prana*), the benefits of proper breathing, the role of the mind in both causing and curing diseases, the energy centers known as *chakras,* and the vital importance of meditation.

The following year, I received another, more severe jolt—again in Scandinavia. On my way to a summer job in Stockholm, a lone tree at the edge of a steep gravel road prevented my skidding car from plunging into a fjord far below. During what seemed like an interminable weekend, I was stuck in a small Norwegian village waiting for transportation, with nothing to do but sit in my room, ponder my stupidity and recklessness (the second serious car accident within a year), and, not least of all, contemplate the preciousness and fragility of life. To keep the panic, fear, and loneliness at bay, I practiced whatever yoga I could remember and spontaneously sat in meditation, surveying myself and examining the incessant stream of thoughts and feelings. It all brought me a surprising and novel kind of calm and inner strength.

A few months after my Norwegian car crash, I happened to buy a book on Buddhism. I was still in my antireligious phase but Zen had piqued my skeptical interest. As I read, I realized in amazement that Zen addressed all the contradictions and questions that other religions and philosophies had engendered. Suddenly all the pieces fell into place and my life was immediately and radically transformed. Buddhism made such utter and complete sense to me that not to live by its teachings seemed foolish and unnecessarily difficult—somewhat like running across a multilane highway for no good reason.

The truth of Buddhist teachings was clear to me: attachment in its many guises is indeed the cause of suffering. I started applying the Buddha's teachings in all areas of my life and experimenting with various forms of meditation, while continuing my extracurricular reading and my martial arts training.

Commitment

After graduating in 1970 I joined an international firm of chartered accountants as an "articled clerk" (basically, an apprentice). I worked during the day, mostly as an auditor, and was expected by my employers to study my correspondence course at night. A lowly articled clerk, I was a fly on the wall as we audited all kinds of businesses across the country—one-person operations, large factories, fashionable hotels, banks, insurance companies, international arms dealers. A necessary part of my job was to interview people at all levels of an operation, from the lowest to the highest, to observe not only formal systems but also personality dynamics. Many of the people I met were eager to have someone listen to them. They talked about business matters and office gossip, told their life stories, and shared their personal philosophies, hopes, and dreams. A common dream was retirement, since many were unhappy in their jobs. Unfortunately for some, their health and/or bank accounts were not robust enough to sustain their retirement dreams.

In hindsight, although my work as an articled clerk was in many ways tedious, it afforded me a very valuable and special opportunity to study the workings of the business world and human behavior in general. I was in the position of a neutral observer, not only because I was an outsider to particular corporations or businesses, but also because I was an outsider to English culture, even though by that time I functioned comfortably enough within it. My experiences during that period also confirmed many of the business, power, and wealth dynamics I had earlier observed in Guyana through my father's business operations and his high-society contacts. All of these personality dynamics and personal histories in turn served to reinforce for me the wisdom of the Buddha's teachings. Beneath the almost universal veneer of "I'm all right" normality, there is widespread pain and suffering. Invariably the cause of such suffering is attachment to some person, desire, expectation, ideal, ideology, religious belief, or the like. Letting go of such attachment is very rarely considered as a course of action.

After only a few months as an articled clerk, I encountered a common workplace dilemma: I hated my job. It made sense in terms of long-term financial security and prosperity to undertake such employment and training, but I could see no inherent life-enhancing value in accounting, and I found the corporate, nine-to-five environment toxic and soul-destroying. It was hard to get through each workday, let alone envision a whole lifetime of such days.

When I realized I was in deep conflict, I decided to test the Buddha's teachings in a real-life situation. I sat in quiet, patient meditation looking for what the Buddha called "clear comprehension of purpose" *(satthakasampajanna)*. After a few days, I found it. It became perfectly clear that, although my situation was not perfect, it was appropriate to finish my qualifications as a chartered accountant since I had no practical alternative at that time. As part of this newfound clarity, I also experienced "acceptance of what is." I took each day and each moment one at a time, doing my job to the best of my ability and, when I left work, mentally setting it down and no longer taking home stress, worry, conflict, and regret. The time at work I had previously experienced as tedious and strained passed much more quickly and painlessly, and my practice of Buddhism deepened. Even my work performance improved.

In hindsight, 1974 was a year of great confluence and synchronicity. At the age of twenty-five, I finally qualified as a chartered accountant; my girlfriend, Yolind, and I decided to get married, despite initial opposition from her father; and I made an inner commitment to study Buddhist meditation more formally, with a group. I had long sought an eminent master with whom to study the Chinese martial arts, and in that same year I was fortunate to meet and begin training with two of them.

After experimenting with various forms of meditation, Buddhist and otherwise, I was drawn back to where I started—*vipassana,* a practice also known as insight meditation, with Zen a close second. My search through the Buddhist Society in London led me to the Thai vipassana master Dhiravamsa, who, together with his friend Chogyam Trungpa, was among the earliest Buddhist meditation masters to be sent to England to teach the Dharma. Dhiravamsa had a very powerful presence, yet he was warm, openhearted, and refreshingly ordinary. He made no attempt to hide his human foibles, which I think he found amusing. Of Trungpa and Dhiravamsa, Anne Bancroft writes, "...both seem to emanate characteristics of serene cheerfulness and calm good sense. This latter quality belongs, in particular, to Dhiravamsa. Although not physically large or imposing..., his personality quietens and brings together a waiting audience. When he addresses groups in his clear careful style, even the most irrational or persistent questioner is transported to an area of practical common sense."[2]

After my very first meditation retreat (with Tew Bunnag, Dhira-vamsa's senior disciple) I started meditating at least once a day and subsequently went on as many meditation retreats with Dhiravamsa as I could manage.

Dhiravamsa believed in thoroughly working through emotional blockages and areas of avoidance (using nontraditional techniques when necessary) rather than treating them as mere impediments on the way to enlightenment. He also emphasized the importance of bringing meditative awareness into ordinary life and relationships, and this was one of the main reasons that I choose him as my teacher. I knew that because of my personality, it was relatively easy for me to sit and meditate quietly for long periods in the traditional manner, but I found expressing emotion much more difficult and challenging. I could see how a meditator might easily mistake repression for transcendence. Dhiravamsa's unconventional approach caused ripples within the British Buddhist community, which formerly had lauded him. He was a teacher ahead of his time.

During that same year I started practicing with two highly respected teachers of Chinese martial arts, the Shaolin master Tan Choo-seng, who was living in Singapore, and Rose Li in London. Miss Li was a renowned master of the lesser-known "internal" martial arts of *taijiquan* (also written *tai chi chuan*), *baguazhang,* and *xingyiquan,* which are generally regarded as being more influenced by Daoism and especially the yin-yang philosophy than the external forms, commonly known as kung fu. I saw her name on the notice board of a small London bookstore, and a quick check indicated that she was the same person I had read about in a book by Robert Smith. Smith, an American who had studied martial arts in the East, was one of the first to write books in English about the internal martial arts.

I went to Miss Li intent on learning the most powerful and direct of the internal arts, xingyiquan ("mind-form fist"), but she insisted I start out with the softest style, taijiquan ("supreme ultimate fist" or "yin-yang fist"), which is generally practiced very slowly. I did not realize at that time how influential taijiquan, and through it Daoism, would eventually become in my life. I started my study of taijiquan with less than full enthusiasm because it seemed too slow and removed from "real fighting," a mistaken attitude, which I as a teacher now commonly encounter.

Even in those early years there was an interplay in my life between Buddhism and taijiquan. Dhiravamsa regarded taijiquan as excellent bodywork to accompany the sitting vipassana meditation during intensive retreats and would occasionally ask me to lead his retreat group through some basic taijiquan drills and movements. Miss Li did not approve of this, as she felt that I was subordinating taijiquan to vipassana. Although I did not agree with her, I could well understand her reasoning and general concern over what she called "chop suey" practices, that is, everything tossed into the same pot and served up with the same flavor.

My meeting up with the Shaolin master Tan Choo-seng was also full of seeming coincidence. At the invitation of my future in-laws, I made my first trip to Singapore and, as was my habit at the time, started to check out all the local martial arts clubs. Shortly after I arrived, I noticed a newspaper story about members of a local Shaolin Quan (literally "Shaolin fist") organization that had gone to a prestigious full-contact fighting tournament in Malaysia and had done extraordinarily well. When I tracked them down, on the flat roof of a modest residential building (just as in the kung fu movies), I was impressed not only with their overall power and speed but with the pride they took in the beauty and grace of their movements. I was also impressed when they politely offered me tea, rather than glaring at me with suspicion and menace, as was more commonly my experience during my visits to unfamiliar martial arts clubs in those early days.

A few days later, my future father-in-law mentioned he had discovered during a casual conversation that his dogs' veterinarian also practiced kung fu. Upon hearing of my interest, the vet invited me to visit his club. I was shocked to find out not only that it was the same club I had just visited, the Hua Tiong Pugilistic Arts Institute, but that the vet, who was high up in their organization, had arranged a personal meeting with their master, Tan Choo-seng. After formalities and small talk, he asked me to show him not my karate and judo, in which I had black belts, but my taijiquan, which I had only just started. He seemed pleased and subsequently offered to give me private lessons, which I could hardly refuse.

I individually trained with Master Tan, barefoot on the sun-baked concrete of his backyard, for about two hours every weekday and then was expected to turn up for his evening group classes as well. If the club was taking part in a demonstration, dragon dance, religious ritual, or the like, I was expected to participate. It was the kind of traditional kung fu practice that I had only ever seen in films and did not know still existed. Many of my fellow students came from colorful (and sometimes shady) walks of life. When I first trained with the Shaolin "eyebrow staff," which is about six feet long (and reaches the eyebrow of a very tall person), I wore the skin off my hands, and every single muscle of my body screamed in agony; when I learned the *tiger coming down the mountain* form, I was expected to jump and roll across my spine on the concrete.

I trained with Master Tan like this for several years, one intensive month at a time. After coming to Canada I gradually lost touch with him, but many years later, in 1995, I bumped into him in a corridor of a Baltimore hotel during the World Wushu (Chinese martial arts) Championships. I was there as a part of the Masters Demonstration Team from Canada, and he was the manager of the Singapore wushu team, which excelled in the championships.

Yolind and I were married in 1975 in Singapore, and in 1976 we took a monthlong trip, mostly by local buses and trains, across the northern part of India. We included several famous spiritual places on our journey, including Varanasi, where many Hindus in their old age go to live a spiritual life, and Sarnath, where the Buddha became enlightened. For me it was a very rich experience, since I was by then familiar with yoga, Hinduism, and of course Buddhism. We got a chance to speak with many local priests and holy men. What struck me most about India was its dusty timelessness and vastness, where one had a sense of births and deaths arising and ceasing, rolling on into eternity. Common daily or material concerns seemed trivial by comparison. Many people in the countryside possessed only a few days' supply of food, yet several householders cheerfully and sincerely invited us to eat with them.

In England, I continued my training with both Dhiravamsa and Miss Li and established close personal relationships with them. In time, Miss Li taught me the other internal martial arts of baguazhang and xingyiquan. My ties with Dhiravamsa's organization in England grew (he was by then living most of the time in Berkeley, California), and I would occasionally co-lead vipassana meditation retreats.

In the latter part of 1981, Yolind and I, expecting our first child, moved to Toronto, where the rest of my family had settled.

Taking the Plunge

I worked in the family business—mostly real estate and investment—in Toronto, but my heart continued to ebb away from the business world, and it got harder to do even simple things. It did not help that the eighties were by then getting into full Free Market swing—property flips, shady business deals, and lots of ostentatious spending. I was disappointed, but not surprised, to learn that many of the flag-waving activists and idealists of the sixties (including many of the prominent revolutionaries at LSE) were riding the crest of this new materialism as CEOs and entrepreneurs.

My other life kept tugging at me. Soon after our arrival in Toronto, a real estate contact introduced me to his martial arts teacher, Sifu Steven Law, who ran a Wing Chun club in the basement of his suburban house. The club was "closed-doors," which meant it required introduction by an existing member. Sifu Law generously invited me to train with him, and I eventually "graduated" in 1984, which was considered an unusually short period. Wing Chun is renowned for its close-quarters hand techniques and straight-line approach. I was fortunate to attend some instructional sessions with Sifu Law's teacher, Wong Shunleung, when he visited us in Toronto. Wong was a senior disciple of Wing Chun grandmaster Yip Man, and both were Wing Chun teachers of the world-famous Bruce Lee.

Out of the blue, during the summer of 1983, Dhiravamsa invited me to train to be a vipassana teacher at his new meditation center on San Juan Island, in Washington State. Although I knew it was a rash decision on my part (I did not have any savings), I immediately accepted his invitation. To me, it was like a lifeline or an unexpected beacon. To most people around me, however, it was craziness, but they bit their tongues—except for my father and older brother, Brian, who thought seriously of dis-inheriting me. They were convinced I was entering a brainwashing cult, although they never actually inquired about what I thought or did.

Our growing family spent just over a year with Dhiravamsa on the beautiful and relatively remote San Juan Island. My typical day started before dawn, meditating with Dhiravamsa, preparing and eating break-fast with him, then moving on to a session of theory or discussion. Often we would discuss the news, books, other teachers, and spiritual paths. Once we simply sat and stared at each other for half an hour, since there was nothing to be said!

I assisted on retreats and helped with administration as well as prop-erty maintenance—gathering and chopping wood, digging ditches, patch-ing roofs. My free time was filled with long walks in the hills and on the beaches, communing with the deer, rabbits, owls, eagles, and whales. I often took our two-year-old daughter, Shuwen, with me to give her mother, who was then pregnant with our second daughter, a break. During this time Shuwei was born, and I finally found the self-confidence to start working on a book explaining in straightforward terms the benefits of meditation in daily life. This eventually evolved into *The Conscious I: Clarity and Direction through Meditation,* which came out in 1992.

After about a year, our money began to run out and we had to figure out what to do next. After much meditation and soul-searching, I decided that I could not go back to the business world. My heart was no longer in it, and my various practices required more time than I could spare while working at a conventional job, especially since we now had two young children to look after.

The only solution I could find was to earn a living as a teacher. I promised Yolind that, whatever happened, we would always have adequate food, shelter, and clothing. We might never get rich from my teaching, but we would have each other, and I would be able to spend more time with her and the children than if I had a regular job. Yolind agreed that it was best for me to follow my heart, but she probably harbored deep concerns and fears about the choice I was making. After all, she had come from a wealthy family and had first met me as a young man-about-town with bright prospects in the conventional world. But here I was, at the age of thirty-five, supporting my small family very modestly and about to plunge into even more precarious financial circumstances.

We returned to Toronto so that I could try to establish myself as a teacher of insight meditation, as vipassana was often known, and taijiquan. These two disciplines were the ones I felt most confident about, and Dhiravamsa and Miss Li had approved of my teaching them. At that time I had no master plan to form the two disciplines into an integrated system. I just enjoyed them, and both benefited me greatly. I wanted to share that.

In Toronto, I didn't know where to start. Not many people were aware of vipassana meditation; *tai chi* classes were common in community centers and the like, but the teaching there was monopolized by a big tai chi organization that used relative novices as teachers. Coincidence struck again. At a health food store I noticed that *Common Ground* magazine had just started up in Toronto, and one of its founders was Ron Rosenthal, who used to run a small health food store where we had lived before leaving for the West Coast. When I called him up to inquire about advertising space in his magazine, he told me he was organizing the first big body-mind-spirit convention/show in Toronto and offered me a special price on a booth. So I set up my booth with a simple sign saying "Tai Chi & Insight Meditation" and ran some video footage of myself doing taijiquan. After the fair was over, I was shocked to discover that the weekend had yielded eighty names of people interested in classes or being on my mailing list! I had enough to start a couple of small classes.

Marketing Self-Transformation

Having accumulated experience in the international business world, I knew that establishing myself as a teacher of taijiquan and vipassana would not be easy. My product was relatively unknown and complex; *I* was unknown; my personality was not suited to selling and marketing, being rather introverted and cerebral. North America is very much a consumer society, even more so than Europe. The many billions of dollars invested by various marketers and advertisers over decades have conditioned us to respond to slick packaging (of both objects and people) and a product that promises quick, measurable results—the proverbial "quick fix," "magic pill," or "miracle method." Most people believe they are unaffected by advertising, but studies have consistently proven that belief to be mistaken.

Although my most immediate market was "alternative" (wholistic health, New Age, Eastern spirituality, martial arts, human potential, etc.), it soon became clear that the same principles applied as in the more conventional marketplace. Many of the successful teachers were celebrities—good looking, charismatic, rich, socially connected, or just excellent marketers—packaging their product or system to make it appear easy, immediate, flattering, exciting, or dramatic for their customers.

Credibility depended on having a famous lineage, being a robed monk, or having a recognizable Western qualification like being an academic, psychologist, nurse, or, best of all, medical doctor. It did not matter that those academic qualifications often had little to do with a particular discipline or field. For example, medical doctors with very little training practice acupuncture, teach meditation or taijiquan, and routinely get an ample number of students not only because of the general reverence accorded them but because they can get their clients reimbursed for their treatments or therapy. Another asset for a teacher in this marketplace is recovery—from alcohol, drugs, obesity, abuse, or anything else. In our present media-driven environment, the story of a victim is considered more interesting than of someone who makes consistent, wise decisions. Unusual or "amazing" events like near-death experiences, visions, and messages from aliens or other channeled beings also sell far better than profound spiritual wisdom from an ordinary, incarnate human being. In our present age, as Marshall McLuhan so astutely observed, the medium is the message.

Both of my main teachers, Dhiravamsa and Rose Li, disapproved of using teaching lineages as selling features, and I found I agreed with this sentiment. When I started teaching, therefore, prospective students did not know much of my background, nor did they understand what it was that I was really teaching, since I stayed away even from labels like "Buddhism" or "Daoism." With hindsight, I can say my teaching was the transformation of the whole being, including consciousness, congruent with the tradition of ageless, Perennial Wisdom—but at the beginning of my teaching experience, I was not able to describe it so succinctly.

My basic approach was to try explain as clearly as possible what I taught and how it was relevant in modern life. I did not ask people for belief but the openness to test it for themselves. We cannot find what is truly appropriate for ourselves if we do not know who we really are in the first place. Investing time now in self-knowledge, while it might seem a waste and irrelevant to "real life," can save us much grief in the long term, after we have tired of the succession of illusionary quick fixes, flavors of the day, and shortcuts.

Change at a deep level will automatically ripple out into all corners of our lives with no additional effort, bringing us simplicity, clarity, and compassion. If individuals were to manage only a marginal upward shift in consciousness (far short of enlightenment) and that shift were to ripple out, eventually it could affect six billion people, the global population, the whole world. Over time, the spiritual tortoise often beats the rabbit. We can start here and now; we don't have to wait until we can live in a monastery or some other exotic "spiritual" place. Indeed the planet is rapidly being shaped in the government offices and corporations of our big cities, and that is where a more enlightened consciousness is most urgently needed.

When I addressed audiences outside of my own teaching organization, the response to my perspective was generally positive—but only a relative few acted on it. Some complained what I was advocating seemed too heavy, negative, removed from "real" life and from their cultural norms. They wanted to experience only the positive, the uplifting, the hopeful, and the easy.

In spite of many obstacles and setbacks, the conviction that it was right for me to teach persisted. Teaching is necessarily also learning. It was healthy for me to keep on challenging my own personality patterns— to risk ridicule and rejection, to open myself more intimately to my students and patients, and to accept the ongoing financial insecurity without fear (at one point, I was paying bills by borrowing on my credit card). One of the best things about my situation was that I could spend almost every day with my daughters, since my teaching was mostly in the evenings.

I managed to attract just enough students to survive financially, and after about five years a small but committed core group of students had gathered. I took some satisfaction in this because I was aware that teachers far more experienced and renowned than I were continually losing students to the many distractions and obligations of modern society. Some very famous tai chi masters were teaching just a handful of students each in San Francisco's Golden Gate Park. And even in Singapore, Master Tan lately had trouble making a full-time living out of martial arts, since his students wanted to "move up" in the modern world and become computer experts, scientists, real estate agents, and stockbrokers. So much cheap entertainment was available that disciplined training began to lose its attraction. Friends and relatives (and occasionally I myself) wondered if I was crazy to be trying to go in the opposite direction. I had academic and business qualifications and connections, but I had given them up to teach a handful of students something obscure and seemingly anachronistic.

I was gratified that this core group did not concentrate on just one practice, but eagerly embraced both vipassana and the martial arts—the yin and the yang, mind and body, passive and active—and they saw that the balanced practices were transforming their lives. These changes included the shedding of excess weight, making long overdue career and relationship changes, improving their physical and emotional well-being, and more.

A strong bond grew between my senior students and me, and we socialized a lot outside of class. I made a deliberate effort to teach more as an older brother or friend than as a remote Master. At that time, I called my organization Emerge Internal Arts, because I saw its function as helping innate abilities and potentials to emerge into consciousness and active life.

More Twists of Fate

My decision to attend one of the first truly national Chinese martial arts competitions, held in Houston in 1989, led to significant changes in my professional and personal life. I was excited by the opportunity to see and interact with practitioners and famous masters of taijiquan and other Chinese martial styles, but at the same time I recoiled from the prospect. Deep inside, I was afraid I might not measure up. I had never even seen a martial arts competition, let alone competed, so I did not know what to expect. Because of my fear of failure, I finally decided to attend as, if nothing else, a spiritual challenge. I promised myself to compete for one calendar year and then stop, whether my results were good or bad.

A whole new world opened up. My competition results (and in subsequent years, those of my students) were very good, especially considering that in those early years competitions attracted the best teachers and their finest senior disciples, so the standard was very high. Even better than the competition results, however, was the opportunity to attend workshops and seminars with teachers renowned not only in North America but in China and Taiwan.

At these competitions I met several teachers who later shared their knowledge and their special expertise with me and with my students. Special mention must be made of the taijiquan master Chungjen Chang of Taiwan (who choreographed and appeared in Ang Lee's film *Pushing Hands*) and Professor Yuzeng Liu of China. When Professor Liu first came into our studio in Toronto, he immediately recognized our organization's logo—Buddhist lotus blossoms surrounding a yin-yang symbol. I thought it was my original creation, but it was a symbol with which he was very familiar in China! Professor Liu was a member of China's National Martial Arts Hall of Fame and also a formal lineage-holder of both the Buddhist Shaolin Temple and the Daoist Wudang system of internal martial arts. He was, in fact, the very embodiment of our organization's logo.

The teacher who had the most dramatic effect on me around this time was Jerry Alan Johnson, a well-known "internal" martial artist who had written several books on the internal arts, including his specialty, baguazhang. We got to know each other during a national convention of baguazhang teachers in 1991. I was struck by the extent of his knowledge and expertise, which encompassed several branches of traditional Chinese medicine including acupuncture and his other specialty, *qigong* (skill in the art of *qi,* or vital energy). He seemed very balanced in his approach, respectful of tradition but not slavish; he embodied the archetypes of both warrior and healer. He also demonstrated an unusual willingness to share his knowledge. When he invited me to visit and train with him at his home near Monterey, California, I unhesitatingly took him up on his offer and a few months later was in California.

What I learned from Jerry Johnson in a relatively short time had a considerable effect on my practice. Much of what he showed me I could do almost right away because I had laid the groundwork with Miss Li and my other teachers—but I had not made certain crucial final connections that integrated everything together. Maybe my teachers hadn't gotten around to teaching me these things, or maybe they didn't know them… or maybe they wanted to keep them secret for reasons of their own.

This integrative knowledge was qigong, which works with body, energy, and mind. I liken it to slotting in the missing pieces of a puzzle, adding detail to a sketch, or making the final electrical connections to complete the construction of a house. This new knowledge in no way negated or contradicted what I already knew, but added detail and dimension. In the next few years, Jerry Johnson regularly came to Toronto to give workshops to my students, not only in the martial aspects of qigong but in medical qigong and energetic healing as well. One of his specialties was dissolving tumors.

In April 1993, a few days short of our second daughter Shuwei's ninth birthday, my wife revealed that she no longer loved or needed me and wanted an immediate separation. This totally unexpected occurence sent shock waves through my personal life and my relationships with my senior students.

By a fortunate "coincidence," I had begun to sit in daily meditation with my three young daughters just a few weeks before this event. Following an especially heated argument between them, it suddenly occurred to me to offer them to do fifteen minutes of standing meditation instead of a much longer period of disciplinary time-outs. To my surprise, they agreed and afterwards remarked that they enjoyed it since it made them feel much calmer and more loving. I suggested that we should sit together every day and they agreed. They were eleven, nine, and six years old at the time. Sitting together in meditation proved to be an invaluable resource and blessing for us all in the following months as we dealt with the resulting loss, hurt, uncertainty, and change. Each of us could go within and acknowledge what was happening, and we could share our feelings and support one another. It was a living lesson in the Buddha's Four Noble Truths, to which I constantly referred as I reminded them to let go of anger, disappointment, bitterness, blame, pain. They described to me what they were thinking and feeling, and occasionally what was happening to them on an energetic level—flows of energy, blockages, sometimes using language like "colors inside." When they held onto emotional pain, they would also feel it as specific physical pain. These were unsolicited and unprompted observations, which made consistent sense to me since I had often worked with students and patients on similar matters and experiences.

Although I expected turbulent times with Yolind and my children, I was surprised by the strong reaction of my senior students to my marriage breakup. It seemed that as their vision of the "perfect couple" crumbled, so did the harmony and cooperation within the core group. It was almost as if it gave them an excuse to "do their own thing," which was to revert to the conditioned, knee-jerk behavioral patterns they were keeping in check. It was amazing (to me) that this occurred, since over the years I had many times explained the dynamics of personality types, identification, and attachments that produce conditioned behavior. I had purposely brought together the conventional opposites—kick-butt macho males and touchy-feely, past-lives women. I had explained yin-yang phi-losophy and the need for an integral practice. I had encouraged the fight-ers to meditate and the meditators to fight. Now both extremes turned against me, finding some kind of ludicrous common cause. Several left, pro-fessing gratitude and love but never contacting me again.

At the time, I felt both alone and embattled. All the work I had done with my students on transcendence, on letting go of attachment and iden-tification, seemed to be shattering against the walls of politically correct dogma: all perspectives are equal; all hierarchies are bad; responsibility and blame in all relationships should be shared fifty-fifty; talk about things and express feelings but don't necessarily make decisions or seek resolutions.

It was not until a copy of Ken Wilber's *A Brief History of Everything* caught my eye in 1996 that I realized this politically correct postmodern morass was a widespread phenomenon. It had its roots in not recogniz-ing and distinguishing between the different levels of consciousness op-erating within us—not acknowledging that not every word or action was in all ways equal in value.

Yet even after this period of discord, about 40 percent of that origi-nal core group of about fifteen is still with me, deepening their personal practice and teaching experience. The senior teachers have been study-ing with me for about fifteen years and have become well-recognized and self-supporting teachers in their own rights, although still working co-operatively within our organization. We now have a younger generation of teachers, the youngest being only twenty-four years old. He started studying taijiquan with us at the age of twelve and has since made much progress in vipassana meditation, baguazhang, and qigong.

Over the years, we have expanded our integral spiritual practices to in-clude not only vipassana meditation, internal martial arts, and bodywork but also the many aspects of (energetic) qigong—spiritual, martial, self-healing, and medical. Those of us who have trained in medical qigong therapy have worked effectively on a wide variety of ailments (including cancer) that were not responding to conventional medicine.

Looking back on thirty-five years of personal practice and twenty years of teaching, I take satisfaction that I have nurtured *gongfu* in myself, my students, and in my children. *Gongfu* is an ancient Chinese term describing work/devotion/effort that has been successfully applied over a substantial period of time, resulting in a degree of mastery in a specific field. Although the term is synonymous in the West with martial arts (though it is most often rendered *kung fu*), it is equally applicable to calligraphy, painting, music, or other areas of endeavor. Our organization's area of expertise is broad—no less than self-transformation on the many levels of being.

Human Potential Movement pioneers George Leonard and Michael Murphy, drawing on their many years of experience working with experts in various fields, also describe the necessity for something akin to *gongfu:*

> In a culture intoxicated with promises of the quick fix, instant enlightenment, and easy learning, it was hard to accept one of the most powerful lessons that came to us out of those powerful but short-term experiences: Any significant long-term change requires long-term practice, whether that change has to do with playing the violin or learning to be a more open, loving person. We all know people who say they have been permanently changed by experiences of a moment or a day or a weekend. But when you check it out you'll generally discover that those who ended up permanently changed had spent considerable time preparing for their life-changing experience or had continued diligently practicing the new behavior afterward.[3]

Although long-term, step-by-step spiritual practice may seem slow and tedious to most people today, it can bring freedom from the pressures of psychological time, simplify the complex, and lead to surprisingly effective action. If we understand ourselves at a deep level, we will also understand others, and this will manifest in a clarity of purpose and action from which we will not be easily distracted. Realizing that we can act only in the present, we take one step at a time, letting go of the compulsion of both past and future. In this undramatic way, we can take each step along the thousand-mile journey with seeming ease. It is easy and simple, yet also not. The sage is always still human and must deal with the inevitable aspects of human experience—disappointments and reversals of fortune and all the rest—like everyone else. We all have a choice about whether to hold on to our pain or let it go.

For all us, both individually and globally, the urgency of a transformation of consciousness is increasingly apparent.

Section II:
The Spiritual
Legacy of Shaolin

2

The Miracle at Shaolin Temple

Sometime between 520 and 527 C.E., it is said an Indian Buddhist monk named Bodhidharma came to the obscure Shaolin Temple on Mount Song in Henan Province, China. He spent at least nine years there and is believed to have died shortly after that period. The Chinese rendered his name as Puti Damo (Damo for short), and later on the Japanese knew him as Bodai Daruma (or just Daruma).

Those nine years at Shaolin proved to be of enormous significance: today Bodhidharma is widely regarded as the founder of two world-renowned traditions. He is honored as the first patriarch of a major and influential branch of Buddhism, "Chan," now widely known and practiced as "Zen," its Japanese name. He is also commonly credited with laying the foundational training for the famous fighting monks of Shaolin, whose heroic deeds over the centuries made Shaolin Quan the most famous system of martial arts in China and influenced local fighting arts throughout the Far East. The Chinese martial arts (commonly called *gongfu* or *wushu*) are currently being practiced and propagated around the world. Offspring like karate and taekwondo are even more popular.

Some sources claim that Bodhidharma was a prince from Kanchipura in southern India and on his journeys through China he met Emperor

Wudi of the Liang dynasty. The emperor was an enthusiastic supporter of Buddhism who built many temples and supported the community of monks. During the interview, the emperor asked Bodhidharma what merit his good deeds would earn him, perhaps hoping for enlightenment. Damo replied, "No merit whatsoever." When the emperor asked him to explain the essence of Buddhism, he simply answered, "Emptiness." These curt and enigmatic replies, which greatly disconcerted the emperor, foreshadowed later Chan teaching methods.

Legends about Bodhidharma abound. On his way to Shaolin Temple he was supposed to have floated over the famous Yangzi River on a leaf (or, in some accounts, a single blade of grass), and this feat is often depicted in paintings and statues. Probably the best-known story concerning Bodhidharma is that he sat for nine years in meditation facing a cave wall, a practice since known as "wall-contemplating" meditation. Elaborations of this legend include the story of Bodhidharma falling asleep during meditation and becoming so frustrated with himself that he cut off his eyelids and hurled them to the ground, where they sprouted into the very first tea plants. Another legend contends that Damo's meditation was so intense that his shadow became imprinted on a rock in the cave. The alleged shadow-imprinted rock can still be seen today at the Shaolin Temple complex.

Although it would be unwise to take these legends literally, they are not necessarily without meaning. For example, D.T. Suzuki, one of the early modern authorities on Zen, characterizes "wall contemplation" not as the practice of meditation facing an actual wall but to a state of mind. He quotes from an early work known as the *Pieh Chi:* "The master first stayed in the Shorinji (Shaolin-szu) monastery for nine years and when he taught the second patriarch, it was only in the following way: 'Externally keep yourself away from all relationships and internally, have no pantings (or hankerings, "chuan") in your heart; when your mind is like unto a straight-standing wall you may enter into the Path.'"[4]

Shaolin Warrior Monks

Legend has it that when Bodhidharma arrived at Shaolin, the monks practicing there were frail and sickly and fell asleep when they tried to meditate. He believed that strong bodies and good health would aid their spiritual practices and supposedly taught them three qigong exercises that are still practiced: the Muscle and Tendon Changing Classic *(yi jin jing)*, Bone-Marrow Washing *(xi sui jing)*, and the Eighteen Lohan Qigong *(shi ba lo han gong)*. There is some disagreement as to whether these exercises were from Indian yogic or Chinese qigong traditions and whether they originated in Bodhidharma's time or later. Whatever the truth may be, however, not too long after Bodhidharma's death Shaolin's first martial hero emerged. Wang Jinnaluo, a humble temple cook, used a wooden staff to single-handedly drive off a band of armed Red Turban bandits who were attacking the temple. His statue stands today, along with Bodhidharma's, in the Song Shan Shaolin Temple.

The Shaolin Temple was first and forever etched in the minds and hearts of the Chinese people when thirteen Shaolin monks played a prominent role in unifying China and establishing the Tang dynasty, fondly regarded as a golden age of chivalry and excellence in the arts, science, and technology.

During the Tang dynasty, which lasted nearly three centuries, the fame of Shaolin monks spread throughout China, attracting those who wanted to study their distinct brand of direct-transmission Chan Buddhism and their amazing martial skills. The temple became one of the main inspirations within China for the novel idea of the chivalrous "spiritual warrior." The spiritual seeker need not shun the world, one's own physical health, or even the fighting arts, because the spiritual battle was recognized as occurring both internally and externally. At the same time, the warrior, instead of being content with ruthless and brutish violence, could aspire to act out of morality, compassion, and spiritual insight. Each

Shaolin monk or lay student had to swear to uphold a strict moral code before he was taught the fighting arts.

The movements of the original Eighteen Lohan qigong (a lohan, or arhat, is one who has reached the stage of nirvana) became the basis of martial training and in time developed into a more complex system of 72 movements. By the time of the Mongol Yuan dynasty (1279–1368), these had expanded to 170. These movements were expressed in the Five Styles, which drew upon the fighting styles, characteristics, and spirits of different animals. The dragon, tiger, leopard, snake, and crane (or cock) styles represented the training of spirit, bones, strength, qi, and sinews respectively. It was said that to truly master this "mimic boxing" (imitating various animals), the human ego had to be set aside, which is also one characterization of the goal of Chan Buddhism.

During the Ming dynasty (1368–1644), Shaolin Temple martial training began to incorporate a variety of weapons (spears, cudgels, swords, iron staffs), partly in response to the increasing incursions and raids by Japanese pirates. Shaolin monks were repeatedly enlisted to help repel the Japanese invaders, and it is recorded that during this period Shaolin enjoyed great favor with the government and with the grateful people of China. By this time the number of Shaolin monks had grown into the thousands.

As early as the Tang dynasty, the influence of the Chinese martial arts, and especially Shaolin Quan, had spread beyond the borders of China, mingling with the local fighting styles, religions, and customs to produce new styles and practices. As Donn F. Draeger and Robert W. Smith explain, "Empty-hand fighting techniques developed in the Tang dynasty were so influential throughout Asia that they became the core of the fighting arts of other neighboring countries. This is shown by the fact that the same Chinese terms were used in Korea, Okinawa, and Japan—though Japan was to change the terms to pave the way for modified physical and philosophical concepts. The original empty-hand fighting method of

Korea, 'tang su,' was derived from Chinese methods. Its very name means 'Tang Hand.'"[5]

Probably the most famous and historically significant product of this intermingling process was the phenomenon of the Japanese *bushi*, better known by a name that developed in the fourteenth century—*samurai*. The Japanese had been borrowing and adapting fighting and weapons systems from China from as early as the beginning of the Tang dynasty. For at least three centuries following the Taika reforms in 645 C.E., however, Japan was ruled by the civil class and enjoyed relative peace. But around the twelfth century the authority of the civil class began to break down, and the military class, the bushi, correspondingly rose in importance. In 1192 Minamoto Yorimota became the first of the *shogun,* a hereditary line of ruthless military dictators that lasted until 1868. Their power rested on the bushi, who, as a warrior class, were considered superior to farmers, artisans, and merchants and were dedicated to carrying out the orders of their overlords *(daimyo)* even unto their own deaths.

The Japanese bushi/samurai were influenced not only by the fighting techniques developed within the Shaolin Temple, but also by the particular brand of Buddhism, Chan, that originated there. Buddhism had been influential in Japan as early as the sixth century, but Chan became familiar to the Japanese much later, at about the same time that the shoguns were coming to power. This new form of Buddhism appealed to the samurai because it was powerful, direct, and not dependent on book learning. It allowed them to fight and face death with equanimity. "The aim of Zen," writes D.T. Suzuki, "is to throw off all the external paraphernalia which the intellect has woven around the soul and to see directly into the inmost nature of our being. Man is not simply a constructed creature; he requires many appendages, but when they grow too heavy he wants to unload himself and sometimes to include his own existence."[6] It must be noted that even during those periods when the samurai were at their most honorable, they tended to use Zen as an utilitarian means to an end, rather than truly embodying its true spirit. Although the samurai were prepared to die for their overlords, they were not free from the conditioning paraphernalia of the elaborate bushido code of conduct, the expectations of society, or the orders of their masters, which might include committing murder and treachery—expressly against the precepts of moral action common to all sects of Buddhism.

The influence of the Shaolin Temple remained strong within China over the centuries. By the early Qing dynasty (1644–1911), there were ten related Shaolin temples scattered throughout China, and many new systems of martial arts were created, often using Shaolin Quan as a foundation or starting point. These included Praying Mantis, taijiquan, xing-yiquan, baguazhang, and tongbeiquan.

Obviously, as modern weapons grew more powerful and long-range, the martial arts became less effective in military conflicts. Within China, the last great attempt to pit traditional martial skills against modern weapons came during the Boxer Rebellion. The European countries' increasing control of trade, often enforced by gunboats and troops, humiliated and incensed the Chinese. The British had successfully fought two opium wars to force the Chinese government to allow them to sell opium and other goods within China. In 1900 nationalist Chinese, led by a secret society called the Society of Harmonious Fists, or "Boxers," rose up against the Western allied forces. The Boxers fought with fists, staffs, spears, and sabers against guns and cannon. Some felt that their qi, their inner energy, would protect them from bullets, while others regarded modern weapons as cowardly, inhuman, and primitive, since they killed impersonally from a distance. Following the predictable defeat of the Boxer Rebellion, the foreign powers assumed even greater power. The Boxer Rebellion, however, produced a new generation of martial heroes including two famous baguazhang masters, Cheng Tinghua and Li Cunyi, who reputedly used their nimble footwork and spinning, circular techniques to defeat multiple opponents at close quarters.

During the twentieth century, the martial arts have remained popular in China, but emphasis has shifted away from military training toward "physical culture": fitness and sports. The Communist governments promoted wushu as a unique form of Chinese gymnastics or art of physical movement and started teaching standardized courses in universities. Any esoteric or spiritual interpretation of these arts was discouraged.

The original Song Shan Shaolin Temple, like the rest of China, experienced much upheaval and hard times during the twentieth century but has now rebounded. It was torched in 1928 during a battle between warlords and again during the Cultural Revolution in the late seventies, after which fewer than ten monks, impoverished but defiant, remained in the ruins of the temple.

China and the rest of the world, however, would not let Shaolin die. It is now rebuilt and, thanks to TV and films—especially the 1982 hit *The Shaolin Temple* starring Jet Li—is a popular year-round tourist attraction. Several wushu schools accommodating thousands of students have sprung up around the temple, making it by far the largest martial arts community in the world. Genuine Shaolin monks, aided by top-ranked wushu performers, give theatrical performances all around the world. Resident monks at the temple, presently numbering about thirty, still train in both Chan and Shaolin Quan. Shaolin's values and heroics now shine and inspire worldwide.

China's Gift to Buddhism

The rise of the warrior-monk tradition was one remarkable occurrence at Shaolin. Another was the development of Chan, the first truly Chinese form of Buddhism, which became one of the jewels of the Mahayana traditions.

Scholars broadly agree that Buddhism began to trickle into China from India shortly after the opening of the Silk Road trading route, between 50 B.C.E. and 50 C.E. Written accounts from as early as 93 C.E.

mention the existence of Buddhist monasteries in China. The Buddha, of course, lived about six hundred years earlier. In the early years, the Chinese tended to regard Buddhism as a foreign form of occultism or an Indian variant of their own Laozi's teachings (Laozi's writings were the foundation of Daoism). Their understanding of Buddhism grew in sophistication as more Buddhist sutras were translated from Sanskrit into Chinese from the second century onward. Among these translations were two sutras that would later play an important part in Chan Buddhism: the Prajnaparamita Sutra, which advocated nonduality, was brought to China in 260 C.E., and the Lankavatara Sutra arrived around 300 C.E.

Chan was known as "a direct transmission of the Buddha's teachings outside of the written scriptures," and in most Chan and Zen lineages Bodhidharma is listed as the First Patriarch.

Some of the earliest extant histories of Chan, however, claim that Bodhidharma's own lineage dated back to the Buddha himself. These early-eleventh-century documents state that Bodhidharma was the twenty-eighth patriarch of an earlier direct transmission Indian lineage. The origin of this assertion is said to be the "Flower Sermon," which the Buddha supposedly gave at a place called Vulture Mountain. Instead of preaching a conventional verbal sermon, the Buddha simply held aloft a flower. No one knew what to make of this gesture except for his senior disciple, Mahakashyapa, who smiled knowingly. The Buddha proclaimed, "I have the most precious treasure, spiritual and transcendental, which this moment I hand over to you, O Venerable Mahakasyapa." It should be noted that the very earliest Chan history, Records of the Transmission of the Lamp, written in 1004, makes no mention of this Flower Sermon transmission. Some scholars speculate that the earlier lineage might have been created to add greater authority to the Chan lineage in China.

The name *Chan* is derived from *chan-na*, which is the Chinese transliteration of the Indian term *dhyana* or *jhana*. Its general meaning in Chinese

Buddhism is "meditation" with an emphasis on discovering and experiencing wisdom and truth.

In the earlier Theravada Buddhism *jhana* has a more specific meaning, implying a trancelike state achieved through intense concentration, or one-pointedness. To reach the higher levels of *samadhi* (concentration), one must pass through several stages of jhana "with form" and then, as concentration intensifies, several "formless" stages of jhana. Scholar and Theravadan monk P. Vajiranana Mahathera writes: "Samadhi in its general characteristic is regarded as twofold: 1) the concentration or collectedness of any kind of pure and skillful thought *(kusala cittekaggata);* and 2) the concentration which is transmuted into the Jhanic states. The former generally implies collectedness in the sense of the concentration of the mental processes upon a single idea, which must always be of a wholesome nature; the latter signifies the supernormal state of the same consciousness, which has passed from the ordinary state of Jhana, and this is what is actually implied by Samadhi in any discussion of Buddhist meditation."[7]

Predating Buddhism, jnana yoga of Hinduism is one of the four major paths to the divine. It is the path of knowledge or wisdom through which one strips away all illusion until one's true nature is recognized and oneness with God, or Atman, is experienced. The other spiritual paths of Hinduism are bhakti yoga, the path of devotion or the heart; karma yoga, the path of selfless service; and raja yoga, an esoteric path somewhat similar to esoteric Daoism.

Chan is undoubtedly a "wisdom" path, and penetrating *prajna,* or intuitive wisdom, became very important within Chan/Zen practices. Masters would often go to startling extremes to push their students beyond the circular meanderings of the intellect and book learning into actual enlightenment. Their methods included seemingly nonsensical riddles, shouts, and even physical blows. D.T. Suzuki writes:

> Zen abhors anything coming between the fact and ourselves.
> According to Zen there is no struggle in the fact itself such as
> between the finite and the infinite, between the flesh and the
> spirit. These are idle distinctions fictitiously designed by the in-
> tellect for its own interests.... When we are hungry we eat, when
> we are sleepy we lay ourselves down; and where does the infinite
> or the finite come in here? Are we not complete in ourselves?....
> Let the intellect alone, it has its usefulness in its proper sphere, but
> let it not interfere with the flowing of the life-stream.[8]

Bodhidharma's immediate successor was his disciple Huike, to whom
he is said to have given a copy of the Lankavatara Sutra. Huike became
the second Chan patriarch, and his successor was Sengcan. The fourth
Chan patriarch was Dayi Daoxin (580–651), significant here because he
was the patriarch during the Shaolin monks' heroics at the beginning of
the Tang dynasty.

Most Chan/Zen histories completely (perhaps ashamedly) ignore the
martial history of the Shaolin Temple, and most books on the Shaolin
martial arts inadequately address its spiritual legacy. One important work
on this topic, Andy Ferguson's *Zen's Chinese Heritage*, mentions Shaolin's
martial history only to deny its significance: "Stories linking Bodhidharma
to the Chinese martial arts or 'gongfu' have no historical basis. No evidence exists of any relationship between Bodhidharma and Chinese martial arts beyond their common connection with Shaolin Temple."[9] It is
interesting, however, that only a few pages after this statement, in his ex-
cerpt on Dayi Daoxin, the book mentions one of the few Zen stories that
I assert has important martial undertones:

> In the thirteenth year of the Daye era of the Sui dynasty [i.e., 617],
> Daoxin and his disciples traveled to Ji Province [modern Jian City
> in Jiangxi Province]. There they came upon a town under the siege
> of bandits. The siege continued for seventy days without letup and

the populace was terrified. Daoxin took pity on the population
and taught them to recite the Mahaprajnaparamita Sutra. When
the bandits looked at the parapets of the city wall, they thought
they saw phantom soldiers and said to each other, "There are extraordinary people in this city. We shouldn't attack it."[10]

This at first seems to be a story about martial arts, but I assert that it
is one of spiritual power that can be added to the legends concerning the
early Chan masters. However, I do not think it would be absurd to speculate that the bandits might in fact have been driven off by some show
or application of martial force, especially since this alleged bandit inci-
dent occurred around the same time (within just three years) as the heroic
battle during which the thirteen Shaolin monks helped secure the fledgling
Tang dynasty. Ferguson also mentions that Daoxin was thought to have
created the first permanent monastic home for Chan, since before his
time most monks were itinerant. This time frame would also coincide
with the emperor's gift of a large tract of land to the Shaolin monastery
in gratitude to the fighting Shaolin monks.

Around the same time that Chan and Shaolin were enjoying impe-
rial favor, one of their greatest patriarchs came to prominence. This was
Hui-neng, of whom Thomas Cleary writes:

> Hui-neng (638–713) is a central figure of Zen Buddhist tradition.
> The last of the early Grand Masters or founding teachers of Zen,
> Hui-neng is popularly considered the founder of the so-called
> Southern School of Zen. Hui-neng characterized his teaching as
> the teaching of immediacy, based on direct insight into the essen-
> tial nature of awareness…. Hui-neng lived during the Tang dy-
> nasty (619–906), which is often considered the apogee of Chinese
> culture. The development of Chinese Buddhism was particularly
> marked during this era, assisted by imperial patronage.[11]

Hui-neng is regarded as the patriarch who finally threw off the remaining vestiges of Indian Buddhism and made Chan totally Chinese.

Joseph Campbell has identified the years about a century after Hui-neng, 841 to 845 C.E., as a crucial period for Buddhism in China and one in which it was dealt an unexpected and devastating blow from which it never fully recovered. When Emperor Wen-zong died in 840, the most powerful court eunuch, Chiu Shiliang, helped put the emperor's brother, Wu-zong, on the throne. Wu-zong immediately started slaughtering those who had been favored by his brother and then turned against Buddhism, which had also been favored. Condemning Buddhism as alien, he threw his support behind the Confucians and the Daoist clergy. According to Campbell, "A Confucian-Taoist reaction brought the leveling of more than 4,600 monasteries, secularization of more than 260,000 monks and nuns, abolition of some 40,000 temples and shrines, confiscation of 1,000,000 acres of fertile Buddhist lands and manumission of 150,000 monastery and temple slaves."[12]

Buddhism did not disappear in China, but the tide had turned against it.

The last Chinese Chan patriarch was the twenty-fifth-generation master, Wumen Huikai (1183–1260), after whom the lineages passed over to Japan and, to a lesser extent, to Korea. Against a background of increasing disintegration and disunity within China, Chan Buddhism became more formalized and organized. Chan monasteries began to include as basic features the Chan lecture *(shang tang)*; the *gongan (koan)*, a story or question the old masters used as a teaching tool; and the *huatou*, an essential word or key phrase that evoked a well-known *gongan*. Thus masters might shout "Wu!" "Mu!" or "Ho!" at students in order to shake them up and facilitate sudden enlightenment. Collections of *gongan* were compiled and used for teaching purposes. Just two centuries after Hui-neng's time, the written word and formalized teaching structures had returned to Chan.

During the late ninth century, Chan began splitting into different schools, eventually five of them, all tracing their lineage to Hui-neng. Three of these disappeared relatively quickly, but two have survived in Japan. The eleventh-generation master Dongshan Liangjie (804–69) was the founder of the Caodong school, which is now known in Japan as Soto. The Linji school was founded by Linji Yixuan, who died in 866. He was a disciple of the famous and unpredictable master Huangbo, who used blows as part of his teaching method. The Linji school survives today in Japan as Rinzai.

During the thirteenth century in China, the Yuan dynasty (1279–1368) was founded by the nephew of the Mongol Genghis Khan, Kublai Khan, and the lineage of Chinese Chan patriarchs shortly thereafter came to an end. The two occurrences were not unconnected. At about this same time, Chan Buddhism (known as Zen) was becoming very popular in Japan, especially among the bushi/samurai warrior class. The rule of the shogun military dictators was established in Japan in the late twelfth century, and this thrust both the samurai and Zen into prominence. The shogun period in Japan lasted for about seven hundred years, and thus Zen had a profound and long-lasting impact in Japan, not only on military and political matters but also on culture and art.

Today Zen is practiced all over the world and has entered the jargon and imagery of popular culture in all kinds of media—yet all this has much of its origin in China at the birthplace of the famous Shaolin fighting monks. Let's examine this in more detail.

3

Why Did Bodhidharma Come from the West?

Zen Buddhism is the product of the Chinese mind, or rather the
Chinese elaboration of the Doctrine of Enlightenment. Therefore,
when we want to narrate the history of Zen, it may be better in
some respects not to go to India but to stay in China and study
the psychology and philosophy of her people and the surrounding conditions that made it possible for Zen to achieve a successful growth in the land of the celestials, always remembering that
it is a practical interpretation of the Doctrine of Enlightenment.[13]

—*D. T. Suzuki*

"What is the meaning of the Bodhidharma coming from the West?" is one
of the more famous gongan/koans within the Chan/Zen tradition. This is
generally taken as a directive to students to inquire into their own true nature, and thus into the essence of Chan Buddhism and enlightenment.

In this book I propose to take Dr. Suzuki's advice (in the epigraph to
this chapter) and broaden the inquiry into the factors and conditions
that made Bodhidharma's short stay at Shaolin so influential in so many
ways. In this chapter, we explore Chan's connection with China's other
main philosophical currents, Daoism and Confucianism, and in the next

chapter we will examine its relationship with China's martial arts and esoteric traditions.

China's "Three Doctrines"

Scholars commonly agree that the culture of modern China is the result
of centuries of interaction between three philosophies/religions—
Confucianism, Daoism, and Buddhism (especially Chan). Confucianism
and Daoism share a bond inasmuch as both originated wholly in China
and exerted their influence as early as the sixth century B.C.E. Buddhism
was imported from India several centuries later. At the same time,
Buddhism and Daoism have much in common, since they both focus on
the individual rather than society and encourage the individual to look
within for right action. Confucianism stresses humaneness and actualizing morality within established social norms.

The sixth century B.C.E. and the few decades thereafter have been referred to as the "Axial Age" because there was an unprecedented explosion
of extraordinary world teachers around that time. India produced the
Buddha (550–480 B.C.E.) and Vardhamana Mahavira (540–468 B.C.E.),
the founder of Jainism. Greece produced Pythagoras (581–497 B.C.E.),
Socrates (470–399 B.C.E.), and Heraclitus (544–480 B.C.E.), who introduced the Hindu Upanishads to Greece. China produced Confucius
(551–497 B.C.E.) and, possibly around the same time, Laozi, the credited
author of the seminal Daoist work *Dao De Jing*. Legend has it that Laozi
was an older contemporary of Confucius and that the two actually met.
The *Dao De Jing* itself was probably set down in writing later, around the
third century B.C.E.

Confucius (Kong Fuzi) is regarded as China's "First Teacher," and his
impact was substantial and enduring; it is unmistakably evident in Chinese
(and generally East Asian) culture even today. He was the first person in
Chinese history to teach large numbers of students in a private setting,
and several of his students later became eminent scholars and teachers.

He is regarded as the founder of China's philosophical tradition, and like Socrates in Greece, he taught informally through discussions and questions. Confucius also taught extensively with quotations from the Six Classics, the repository of ancient China's culture and wisdom.

The Six Classics, or Six Arts, were the *Yi Jing* (Book of Changes), *Shi Jing* (Book of Odes), *Shu Jing* (Book of History), *Li Chi* (Book of Rites or Rituals), *Yue* (Book of Music and Poetry), and *Chun Qiu* (Spring and Autumn Annals, a history of Confucius's home state of Lu). Of these, only the *Yi Jing* (also transliterated *I Ching*) is reasonably well known in the West. Its sixty-four hexagrams have become a popular source of divination and guidance.

The renowned modern Chinese scholar Fung Yu-lan writes of Confucius that "he wanted his disciples to be 'rounded men' who would be useful to state and society and therefore he taught them various branches of knowledge based upon the different classics. His primary function as a teacher, he felt, was to interpret to his disciples the ancient cultural heritage. That is why, in his own words as recorded in the *Analects,* he was 'a transmitter not an originator.' But this is only one aspect of Confucius.... while transmitting the traditional institutions and ideas, Confucius gave them interpretations derived from his own moral concepts."[14]

One of Confucius's most famous original concepts was "rectification of names." He felt that a prerequisite of an orderly society was that everyone should act in accordance with his name (i.e., his role) in society. "Let the ruler rule, the minister minister, the father father and the son son." Although one should act in accordance with the *yi* (righteousness or "oughtness") of a situation, it was even more important to be guided by *ren* ("human-heartedness" or benevolence). Huston Smith explains Confucius's human-heartedness as "a feeling of humanity towards others and respect for oneself, an individual sense of the dignity of human life wherever it appears. Subsidiary attitudes follow automatically: magnanimity, good faith and charity. In the direction of *ren* lies the perfection of everything that would make one supremely human. In public life it prompts untiring diligence. In private life it is expressed in courtesy, unselfishness and empathy."[15]

A concept like human-heartedness is quite remarkable given the circumstances of Confucius' time—continual, bloody, increasingly brutal warfare and a society rigidly divided into nobles, commoners, and slaves. Confucius championed the cause of the common people and compassionately interacted with people of all different classes.

Confucius was glorified by the Chinese after his death, and within a few generations his teachings began to mold Chinese thinking, government, and culture. This ancient social framework has served China well for more than two millennia. The Chinese have been commonly characterized as family oriented, hard-working, down-to-earth, proud of their history, and possessed of a strong sense of correct or appropriate behavior. Many of these traits can also be observed today in neighboring countries like Taiwan, Japan, Korea, and Singapore. Confucius's teachings are still widely studied in schools and universities today, especially in the Far East.

Philosophical Daoism

China's other early and great inspiration was Daoism. Whereas Confucianism may be characterized as this-worldly and concerned with society's rules, Daoism is other-worldly and looks beyond society. The earliest Daoists, dating back about four thousand years ago, were recluses, refugees, shamans, and the like who shunned conventional society, which they felt was becoming chaotic and plagued by ongoing military conflict. They did not want to get entangled in man-made complexity and craziness but preferred to act in harmony with nature and explore their own inner potential.

The foundation of philosophical Daoism and one of the world's true treasures is the *Dao De Jing*, often translated as "The Way and Its Power."

In this chapter, references to "Daoism" will be to philosophical Daoism as opposed to the other two forms of Daoism, the esoteric and the religious-popular, which will be discussed later.

Fung Yu-lan repeatedly points out the differences between the philosophical and religious aspects of Buddhism and Daoism. The philosophical schools were mostly in agreement, while the Buddhist and Daoist religions competed:

> I must emphasize the distinction between *Fojiao* and *Foxue,* that is, between Buddhism as a religion and Buddhism as a philosophy. Buddhism as a religion did much to inspire the institutional organization of religious Taoism...[which] grew as an indigenous substitute for Buddhism and in the process borrowed a great deal including institutions, rituals and even the form of much of its scriptures, from its foreign rival.... Whereas the Taoist religion was almost invariably opposed to the Buddhist religion, Taoist philosophy took Buddhist philosophy as an ally. Taoism is less other-worldly than Buddhism. Nevertheless, some similarity exists between their forms of mysticism.[16]

Tradition states that the author of *Dao De Jing* was Laozi (literally "old master"), who was allegedly born around 604 B.C.E. and thus would have been a contemporary of Kong Fuzi. Unlike the latter, he was not well known, had no students, and did not consort with nobility. Legend relates that Laozi jotted down what would become the *Dao De Jing* at the request of a humble gatekeeper, who was intrigued by the fascinating old man riding a water buffalo toward Tibet in order to seek greater solitude. Some scholars contend that there were multiple authors of the *Dao De Jing*—which was actually set in writing centuries after the legendary Laozi's supposed lifetime.

Fundamental to the *Dao De Jing* are the concepts of *dao* and *yin-yang*. Although they are now associated with the Daoists, these are native

Chinese concepts that predate both Kong Fuzi and Laozi, appearing in the Book of Changes *(Yi Jing)* and in the Yellow Emperor's Classic of Internal Medicine *(Huang Di Nei Jing Su Wen)*, which forms the basis of traditional Chinese medicine. Huang Di, the Yellow Emperor, is said to have lived during China's prehistoric Legendary Period (2852–2205 B.C.E.), but modern scholarship dates the written *Nei Jing* to 1000–200 B.C.E.

The first chapter of the *Dao De Jing* declares:

> A Way can be a guide, but not a fixed path;
> names can be given, but not permanent labels.
> Non-being is called the beginning of heaven and earth;
> being is called the mother of all things.
> Always passionless, thereby observe the subtle;
> ever intent, thereby observe the apparent.
> These two come from the same source but differ in name;
> Both are considered mysteries.[17]

Although *dao* literally means "way" or "path," it seems similar to what in other wisdom traditions is called the Absolute, god, ultimate reality, ground of being, or Spirit. It is the source of everything and animates and orders everything, but at the same time is indescribably greater than its parts. It is therefore transcendent (not confined to shape and form) and ineffable (beyond the scope of words) as well as immanent (abiding in all things). Thus a person, rabbit, snake, and rock are all part of the Dao, although each does not necessarily possess the same level of consciousness. The recognition of the Divine as both immanent and transcendent is common to all the so-called Ageless or Perennial Wisdom forms of spirituality including Hinduism, Daoism, Buddhism, and the mystic sects of western religions such as the Christian Gnostics, Islamic Sufis, and Jewish Kabbalists. By contrast, popular religion tends to acknowledge only the transcendent aspect of God—separate from and superior to ourselves.

The *Dao De Jing* tells us that the creation-manifestation process tends toward proliferation and complexity, but that all "apparent distinctions" emanate from the same source and share a oneness and interdependence:

> The Way produces one;
> one produces two;
> two produce three;
> three produce all beings:
> all beings bear yin and embrace yang,
> with a mellowing energy for harmony.

The concept of qi (here translated as "energy") figures prominently in esoteric Daoism and Chinese medicine (and both of these will be discussed later), but at this point we will concentrate on the characteristics and dynamics of *yin* and *yang*. The Chinese regard yin and yang as two primary, seemingly opposite forces that manifest within nature and life generally—light and shade, heat and cold, dry and wet, active and passive, hard and soft, male and female, heaven and earth. Although yin and yang appear to be opposites, the Chinese recognize that they are interdependent, transform into each other (when they go to extremes), are ever changing, and yet, underneath all their apparent change and movement, remain the same in their source, which is none other than the Dao. Thus, within yin-yang, there is no absolute, inseparable gulf between good and evil, or man and woman, or any other traditionally opposed pair. Each shares some characteristics and qualities associated with the other; each requires the other for existence. When one side goes too far in opposing the other, it begins to resemble the other. Action causes reaction; "reversing is the motion of Dao." The *Dao De Jing* points out that as soon as there is the concept of good, evil comes into being; if there is beauty, there is automatically ugliness. These dynamics are unmistakably operating right here and now, twenty-five centuries after Laozi, with opposing sides each claiming to be the good and intent on wiping out the evil. President

Ronald Reagan branded the U.S.S.R. the "Empire of Evil" in the Capitalism versus Communism conflict, and President George W. Bush and Osama bin Laden, the Islamic terrorist, labeled each other as "evil."

The concepts of *dao* and *yin-yang* stand in marked contrast to the way in which opposites have been regarded in Western culture. Indeed, Joseph Campbell writes that this is one of the main differences between Eastern and Western perspectives, and is especially important in the way people think in the west about the epic struggle of good and evil:

> For the West, the possibility of such an egoless return to a state of soul antecedent to the birth of individuality has long since passed away; the first important stage in the branching off can be seen…[in] Sumer, where a new sense of separation of the spheres of god and man began to be represented in myth and ritual about 2350 B.C.…. [T]he new mythology brought forth a development away from the earlier static view of returning cycles. A progressive, temporally oriented mythology arose, of a creation, once and for all, at the beginning of time, a subsequent fall and a work of restoration, still in progress. The world was no longer to be known as a mere showing in time of the paradigms of eternity, but as a field of unprecedented cosmic conflict between two powers, one light and one dark.[18]

It is disturbing that in our own era of awesome technological power, certain world leaders still use the simplistic terms of doing battle with evil—which of course is always someone else. We can never reach a truly united collective action, so urgently needed to heal our planet and ourselves, if yang is forever seeking to wipe out yin, or vice versa. The reality, which we can directly ascertain by looking within ourselves, is that yin and yang are interrelated and have a common source which is the Dao.

The *Dao De Jing* concludes that the Sage must act in accordance with the Dao and, to do this, must understand and implement the practice of *wu wei,* or "non-action." Non-action does not mean doing nothing; it means not opposing what is *natural.* This leads to spontaneous, simple, and appropriate action in each and every moment. If we take one such step at a time, we can complete the daunting and great thousand-mile journey.

Laozi warns against confusing yourself with too much knowledge ("Do away with learning, and grief will not be known"), indulging in excessive stimulation ("The five colors will blind a man's sight"), prematurely forcing issues, and getting caught up in apparent opposites. Ironically, all of these practices against which Laozi warns us are prominent in current popular culture, which is fascinated with "winners," excess, youth, physical beauty, and aggressive force. We do not notice (or care) that our idols are discarded when they lose, age, or simply lose their novelty appeal; we fail to recognize the backlash that is generated by brute force, obsession with youth (the fear of aging), and so on.

Contrasting the teachings of Laozi and Confucius, Fung Yu-lan writes:

> Laozi despised such Confucian virtues as human-heartedness
> and righteousness, for according to him these virtues represent a
> degeneration of *Dao* and *De* [power]. Therefore he says: "When
> the *Dao* is lost, there is *De.* When the *De* is lost, there is human-
> heartedness. When human-heartedness is lost, there is righteous-
> ness. When righteousness is lost there are ceremonials. Ceremonials
> are the degeneration of loyalty and good faith and are the begin-
> ning of disorder in the world." Here we find the direct conflict
> between Taoism and Confucianism.[19]

The *Dao De Jing* likens the "highest goodness" to water. Water is soft and yielding, accommodating itself to all circumstances and environments and flowing down to even the lowest of places. Yet life cannot exist without water. Even in its gentle state, it can dissolve the hard—a trickle of water in time will dissolve a mighty mountain. Water not only accommodates change but also can itself change. It can be a raging river, a towering tidal wave, a massive iceberg, or a scorching jet of steam.

The *Dao De Jing*'s advice regarding government is essentially that less is more. A leader of a state needs to act in accordance with Dao in the same manner as an individual Sage. The use of force, trickery, and complex stratagems is seen as self-defeating:

> Governing a large nation
> is like cooking a small fish....
> The more taboos there are in the world
> the poorer the populace is;
> the more crafts people have,
> the more exotic things are produced;
> the more laws are promulgated,
> the greater the number of thieves.

Buddhism and Daoism Meet

It may be said that Buddhism grew out of Brahmanism, as a reaction against the corruption, complexity, superstition, and misunderstanding that had entangled and constricted a great spiritual tradition. The Buddha sought to cut through to the essentials of ageless wisdom, which is none other than the attainment of enlightenment. In the higher levels of enlightenment, the individual no longer feels separate from the Absolute, the One, Spirit, or Dao, which as we have seen is both transcendent and immanent. The name *Buddha* means "awakened one" and speaks volumes about the purpose and focus of his teachings.

The Buddha was spurred on his personal spiritual quest by the universal suffering of all beings, especially human. Once he discovered the cause of suffering and how to remove it, he tried to convey it as directly as possible. He did not discuss anything (including metaphysical speculation about the afterlife) that did not contribute to the individual's liberation from suffering. He stated plainly that he was a mortal human being, but one who was perfectly enlightened. He taught that such enlightenment was within the capability of all people.

Ever focused on simplicity and making himself understood by his listeners, the Buddha summarized his teachings in his Four Noble Truths. The first is that life contains *dukkha* (suffering); second is that the cause of suffering is *tanha*, which has been translated as thirst, desire, craving, or attachment; the third is that the cessation of tanha leads to the cessation of dukkha, which is the complete liberation of nirvana (this is also known as *tanhakkhaya* or the "extinction of thirst"); and the Fourth Noble Truth is the Noble Eightfold Path, which leads to the cessation of dukkha. The Path consists of Right Understanding, Right Thought, Right Speech, Right Action, Right Livelihood, Right Effort, Right Mindfulness, and Right Concentration.

In terms of the First Noble Truth, it must be noted that dukkha is not simply "suffering" or pain but carries connotations of impermanence and insubstantiality. In the West today where "stay positive" is a mantra, the idea of suffering is often dismissed as negative. The Buddha did not say, "Life is a bummer," or that it is not worth living; he said that we suffer because there is in reality nothing or no one solid that we can grasp, since everything is in the process of change. Can you predict how you or your beloved will think or feel about each other a year from now, or be absolutely certain that you will not lose a job, get seriously ill, or suffer a crippling accident? Our present obsession with youthfulness and consequent fear of aging is one example of dukkha. The aging process is perfectly natural, but we suffer because we cannot accept our changing appearance and diminishing physical capabilities, so attached are we to certain ideas (largely fed to us via the media) of how we should look and feel. If we truly accept aging, a wide variety of so-called problems connected with the aging process will simply disappear.

It is interesting that for nearly a hundred years modern science has recognized the fact of constant change and lack of solidity at the atomic and subatomic levels. The universe is not a collection of independent, solid objects that occasionally crash into each other; it is more like an ocean of flowing, changing, interconnected energies and relationships. Yet the dynamic and textured interrelationships of life have penetrated wholly into the popular consciousness, and even basic causes and effects— the effect of pollution on the biosphere, of media on individual decision making, and so forth—are routinely denied or ignored.

The Fourth Noble Truth, the Eightfold Path to nirvana, may be broken down into three main components, subgroups, or "essentials": morality *(shila)*, concentration *(samadhi)*, and wisdom *(pañña* or *prajna)*. It is common to regard shila as the first step, samadhi as the second, and pañña as the final one, but in fact all three may be cultivated at the same time since they support each other. Shila, which has much in common with the moral injunctions of other major religions, is traditionally associated with the heart—compassion for all beings. Compassion and wisdom are regarded in Buddhism as twin virtues necessary for a successful journey along the Path.

Around 100 B.C.E., a new form of Buddhism, called *Mahayana* ("great vehicle"), began to emerge. The original form of Buddhism, as described above, has long been called, somewhat derogatorily, *Hinayana* ("small vehicle") Buddhism. It is now more commonly identified as *Theravada* ("Way of the Elders"). The Theravada ideal is the arhat, who seeks and eventually attains personal liberation *(nirvana)*, often within a simple and secluded environment as a renunciate.

In contrast, the Mahayana ideal is the *bodhisattva,* who in spiritual attainment is the equal of the arhat but who has taken a vow to postpone full enlightenment in order to stay in the world and help all sentient beings find liberation. Mahayana Buddhism sees human beings as very much interconnected and interdependent, not only with one another but also with the whole of the universe. On our path toward enlightenment and liberation, we can both give and receive assistance. Thus the virtue of compassion was greatly emphasized in Mahayana Buddhism, and spirituality became more attuned to the layperson rather than just the monastic recluse. Priests married and had families, religious rituals developed, and metaphysical speculation spread.

An important concept that developed within several Mahayana sects is *shunyata*, the emptiness or nonbeing that underlies all manifestations of forms. D.T. Suzuki writes: "As long as we stay with relativity, we are within a circle; to realize that we are in a circle and that therefore we must get out of it in order to see its entire aspect presupposes our once having gone beyond it. The experience of Emptiness has been there all the time when we began to talk about relativity. From Emptiness we can pass to relativity, but not conversely.... It is the Prajna that sees into all the implications of Emptiness, not the intellect or Vijnana.... If the Mahayana system were built upon the idea of relativity, its message would never have called out such responses as we see in its history in India, China, and Japan."[20]

By the time Bodhidharma arrived at Shaolin Temple, the stage had been set for an extraordinary and unique confluence of Indian and Chinese culture, philosophy, spirituality, and medicine. Buddhism was by then over a thousand years old, and it was suffering from the same kinds of entanglement and loss of vitality that had afflicted Brahmanism in the Buddha's era. Arcane philosophical debate and political maneuvering preoccupied the Buddhist hierarchy, especially within the Mahayana sects.

For their part, the Chinese had also been stagnating after a millennium of the Confucian-Daoist dynamic. They were ready to be inspired and uplifted, especially since the Sui dynasty (581–618 C.E.) had reunited China for first time in more than three hundred years. The Sui emperors undertook ambitious construction and irrigation projects like the rebuilding of the Grand Canal, which linked some of China's main rivers, thereby making north-south travel easier and safer than the sea route, which was plagued by pirates. All this resulted in growing prosperity and expectations.

This great awakening of China coincided with the spread of Chan Buddhism, after Bodhidharma's teaching at the Shaolin Temple around 520–30. Chan was popular because it was a distinctly Chinese form of Buddhism that no doubt bore some resemblance to Daoism. It was down-to-earth, straightforward, and urgent; it deliberately shunned endless book learning and circular intellectual discussion.

The practical and prosaic Chinese, while fascinated by Buddhist psychological insights, metaphysics, and in particular the notion of enlightenment, were more concerned with how those concepts could be put to use in this lifetime rather than in unknowable subsequent ones. In time, Chan developed the concepts of sudden enlightenment and direct transmission, and of living an enlightened but outwardly ordinary life in the everyday world. The final picture in the famous series Ten Cow-Herding Pictures, which depicts the stages of spiritual attainment, shows the enlightened sage reentering ordinary life—"Bare-chested and barefooted, he comes out into the marketplace."

Mahayana Buddhism and Daoism, even as they sparked and challenged each other with their differences, shared several similar ideas and attitudes. Both acknowledged constant change as an important fact of life; they both advised individuals to look within themselves for understanding and appropriate action. Buddhism stressed nonattachment and emptiness *(shunyata)*, while the Daoists talked of non-action *(wu wei)* and nonbeing or emptiness *(wu)*. Both realized that the Absolute Truth or Reality, whether called Dao or nirvana, is beyond words and description.

Many historians and scholars regard the introduction of Buddhism, and especially Chan, as being among the most important events in Chinese history, influencing especially religion, philosophy, art, and literature. Buddhism became the official religion of China in 594 C.E., during the Sui dynasty and, led by Chan, continued to grow and shine during most of the three hundred years of the Tang dynasty that followed, often regarded as China's most brilliant era.

Chan played an important role in helping Mahayana Buddhism spread throughout the Far East, especially to Korea, Japan, and Tibet. By stripping Mahayana Buddhism to its essentials, jettisoning excess intellectual and cultural baggage, Chan made it easier for Buddhism to be adapted to different cultural environments. Even today Chan, in the form of Zen, is in the forefront of a global Buddhist expansion.

In Tibet, the intermingling of this reformed and revitalized Mahayana with local customs and religions resulted in the flowering of the third great branch of Buddhism—Vajrayana ("Diamond Vehicle"). Vajrayana Buddhism, also known as Tantric Buddhism, will be discussed later.

Breaking Through to Enlightenment

If Suzuki is correct in describing Zen as the "Chinese elaboration of the Doctrine of Enlightenment,"[21] a further examination of both enlightenment and the Chinese contribution to it will help us better understand Zen or Chan.

While enlightenment is central to all forms of Buddhism, the possibility of specifically transforming consciousness was a novel concept to the Chinese. Laozi described in general terms how the Sage, or follower of the Dao, might act, but he did not explain in specifics how the ordinary person might become a sage and what internal obstacles there might be. As we shall see later, many Daoists, in their efforts to become sages, concentrated their efforts of conserving and increasing their qi in the hopes of longevity and immortality.

Although the Buddha's Noble Eightfold Path amply spelled out the eight types of right practice needed to take us to enlightenment, it is easy to get caught up in the pursuit of enlightenment and in so doing lose the sense of urgency and immediacy of our daily lives. We try hard, learn ever more, and "make progress," but we never get there because we still envision enlightenment as being some time in the far-off future and maybe in some distant, exotic place. Perhaps we are waiting for a special savior or guru to lead us there.

It has been historically common for Buddhists to visualize and follow the Path in a more or less linear manner—control your behavior, then meditate and try to experience trance states *(jhana)* and, finally, obtain wisdom, which will take you to enlightenment. Some Buddhists undertake just the moral precepts and figure that they will complete the rest of the Path in subsequent incarnations; some insist that completely "stilling the mind" is necessary before approaching wisdom; some feel that wisdom will automatically come through studying the scriptures, listening to Dharma teachings, and performing rituals.

In some ways, Chan was a sharp reminder that Buddhism is essentially about enlightenment and that enlightenment is impossible without wisdom. In Buddhism, prajna is not mere intellectual knowledge accumulated over time but direct wisdom-insight, which dispels ignorance, frees us from the illusory notion of being an ego-entity, and promotes compassion within us. How can we not be compassionate if we directly see (and not just believe) that all beings are interconnected and share an underlying oneness? In the Sutra of Hui-neng, a special section is devoted to explaining prajna:

> The extent of the mind is so vast it pervades the cosmos. When it is used so that it functions adaptively with comprehensive clarity, it knows everything. Everything is one, the one is everything. Going and coming freely, the substance of mind without blockage—this is prajna. Good friends, all prajna insight comes from our own essential nature; it does not enter from outside. Don't misuse your thought and call that the inherent function of intrinsic essential nature…. always acting insightfully and wisely, this is the application of prajna. A moment of folly and prajna is cut off; a moment of wisdom and prajna arises.[22]

Even though at the popular religious level Buddhism and Daoism were rivals, Bodhidharma and his successors at Shaolin Temple obviously found in philosophical Daoism many extremely useful concepts that would make Chan more appealing to the Chinese. These also gave Chan a more urgent and straightforward quality.

Long before Chan, Laozi pointed out that morality and intellectual learning alone were not sufficient for truly living a life according to the Dao and that sometimes they become impediments. We lose sight of the fact that all apparent opposites are interdependent and share an underlying oneness. The more we try to manipulate the world according to our likes and dislikes, the more confusion and complexity we generate, a fact that is all too obvious in our current society:

> When the Great Way is deserted,
> then there is humanitarian duty.
> When intelligence comes forth
> There is great fabrication....
> Eliminate sagacity, abandon knowledge,
> And the people benefit a hundredfold.

The Daoist text above can easily be interpreted in Buddhist terms. If we stay within the ordinary human level of good/bad, pain/pleasure, we will certainly bind ourselves onto the Wheel of Birth and Death *(samsara)*, endlessly and futilely trying to grasp the good and escape the bad. This is the Buddha's Second Noble Truth: we suffer because we are attached to people, objects, ideas, emotions, sensations. Since, however, everything (including the self) is impermanent and insubstantial, they all slip through our fingers. Satisfaction is momentary.

This does not mean one should not experience pleasure or that pleasure is "bad" or "sinful." It is the attachment that causes us suffering and prevents us from adapting to changing circumstances. If we examine our current problems, collective and individual, we will probably observe that most of them arise from the fact that we cannot let go of our haphazardly acquired beliefs, attitudes, and expectations. Even though we may be materially comfortable and physically healthy, many of us suffer merely because we do not have what some others have or as much as we ourselves had at some previous time; we cannot contemplate the possibility of moving beyond being black, white, Democratic, Republican, Christian, Jewish, Islamic, capitalist, and the like. "Stress," which is now a major health hazard in the "developed" world, is an "adaptation disease" in the sense that it arises because we are not adapting appropriately to changing circumstances because we are too rigid or, in other words, conditioned and attached.

The Buddha pointed out that the way to escape the cycle of pain-pleasure and birth-death-rebirth is to break the linkage by letting go of our compulsions and addictions. This is nonattachment, which is also the way to ultimate enlightenment.

The Daoists did not go into psychological and metaphysical analysis as did the Buddhists, but ended up with a similar recommendation for living—wu wei (non-action), which is natural and simple action, undistorted by the calculating mind and self-serving motives. Laozi noted that life is continual change and if we are to flow with change we must be fluid and adaptable like water. He associated the qualities of rigidity and hardness with death and softness and tenderness with the living. The Buddhists would associate rigidity with compulsion, grasping, and attachment.

In order to let go of compulsion through nonattachment, we must be aware or mindful of what is taking place within ourselves each and every moment. In other words, we must practice what the Buddha called Right Mindfulness. If we are not mindful, our conditioned patterns of thought, feeling, and behavior will continue running our lives on "automatic pilot," projecting from past to future and often neglecting the present. Today, in our fast-paced, competitive, multitasking lives, many see this process as admirable, even (grandiosely) heroic—the "urban warrior" running faster and harder than others, trying to manipulate or beat the system.

Many people today feel uncomfortable doing something slow paced and impatient with or dismissive of something that seems to offer no immediate or concrete ("measurable") benefit. Emptiness just does not compute. We can observe this fear of inactivity throughout the popular media, which ever seeks the new, different, and sensational. In truth, much of this is merely the recycling of the mediocre.

I see it in the many students passing through our taijiquan, qigong, and meditation classes. It seems that, while increasing publicity is leading to greater numbers of superficially interested students, the general attention span is shortening. We take on so many activities that we have no time to figure out what they really mean, but somehow we hope to stumble onto something miraculous if we try more and more. What if this "something," however, requires *not* doing, not planning, not grasping, not expecting? What if it is here and now but we simply do not recognize it because we are so busy? What if it lies in the passive yin approach rather than the active yang?

Chan followers found in the *Dao De Jing* parallel concepts to the Buddhist notions of Right Mindfulness and Right Action. If you pay full attention to the challenges and demands of the present, you can resolve problems while they are manageable and easy. If you do not pay attention or put them off because you are too distracted chasing far-off dreams, those problems may build into something complex and overwhelming. In trying to force life to conform to your own arbitrary expectations and desires, you will cause complications and hardships for yourself and others. Acting wu wei, without ambition and attachment to results, you can achieve what is great.

In a similar manner, although within a much more limited context, some of greatest baseball players talk about taking one moment at a time and not overthinking: "See ball, hit ball."

The Chan masters also seemed to have borrowed from the Daoists in formulating and implementing their ideas of sudden enlightenment and direct transmission. The masters did not claim that they had the power to enlighten their disciples, since they were well aware that even buddhas can only *point* the way. When certain students had done sufficient moral and mental preparation, however, the masters would try to push them to the point where they would be able to leave behind the security of the conceptual mind and jump into the unknown, where subject and object, experiencer and experienced all become one.

Unconventional sudden enlightenment methods by the Chan masters might include silence, simply pointing to the ordinary or natural, shouts, unpredictable shock tactics, and even physical blows. Such methods are characteristic not so much of the traditionally controlled and restrained Buddhists but of the colorful and mysterious Daoist recluses, who often lived outside society and its rules. According to Thomas Cleary, these included shamans; herbal healers; diviners; "so-called lost people, descendents of refugee colonies founded by people of vision fleeing ancient wars, taking extended families, even whole villages, along with them; individualists, special people who were known to others but lived independently outside conventional society; and so-called sublimated or spiritualized people, who were believed to be generally unknown to ordinary humanity yet able to exert a mysterious influence under certain conditions."[23]

Zen, Vipassana, Yoga

Although the Chan/Zen masters quite rightly stressed the importance of prajna and enlightenment and their methods were brilliant, colorful, and dramatic, this does not mean that Theravada Buddhism was or is inadequate.

When I first began to read about Buddhism, I was drawn in particular to two forms of practice, Zen and vipassana meditation. The latter is associated with the Theravada tradition and today is often called "insight meditation" because the Pali verb *vipassati* means to see through or to penetrate an object or situation so thoroughly that clear, doubtless insight arises. In defining *vipassana,* Pali terms such as *pañña (prajna)* and *ñana-dassana* (knowledge and vision) are often used. Traditional literature states that when a vipassana practitioner becomes more advanced, he or she will clearly see the truth of the three characteristics of all manifestation—impermanence *(anicca),* insubstantiality or absence of self *(anatta),* and suffering *(dukkha).*

Vipassana practice, based on the Buddha's Sutra on the Foundations of Mindfulness, is simple but profound. The practitioner dispassionately observes whatever is taking place within consciousness but without any identification, desire, or interference. This is much trickier than it may first appear because the need for purpose and achievement is so strong within us. The ego or individual self cannot achieve enlightenment because it is caught in its own circuitous conditioning. It must let go of its control if the enlightenment process is to take place. After a few years of reading and experimentation in various forms of meditation (including non-Buddhist), I decided to make a commitment to Buddhism, eventually choosing vipassana over Zen. My intuitive feeling was that vipassana and Zen were the same in essence but that vipassana was the "yin" expression and Zen the "yang."

I was very attracted by the stories of the Zen masters, the brilliant books of modern master D.T. Suzuki, Zen aesthetics, and Zen's connection to the martial arts. At the same time, I was somewhat put off by its formality and rigidity, which seemed to be at odds with the robust and reckless teachings of its early masters. The Japanese cultural imprint on Zen is very strong, as it is on karate, which I was also learning. I had several friends who were experienced Zen practitioners, and they too emanated a subtle rigidity as well as a certain kind of asserted superiority. My inquiry into Zen included several meditation and discussion sessions at various Zen temples and groups.

I was drawn to vipassana because of its simplicity and lack of manipulation or interference, its non-action—very much like wu wei. Even though I was in my mid-twenties and reveling in the vigorous fighting arts of Shaolin Quan, judo, and karate, I sensed that I needed something softer and more vulnerable as a balance or counterpoint. Vipassana was far less glamorous than Zen, being part of the Theravada tradition, but I felt it was probably more suitable to a busy, modern lifestyle, since it required much less structure.

After I made my choice, I read comparatively little, as my focus was always on personal practice and subsequently on teaching, rather than scholarship. Looking back over the last thirty years, however, I am surprised that my present views are still very much the same as they were back then, except for the fact that I have accumulated various experiences, knowledge, and expertise that enable me to articulate my views a little more coherently and place them in a wider historical and philosophical context.

In exploring the roots of Chan and vipassana, I have found it useful to go back to early Hinduism, out of which Buddhism emerged. As mentioned above, there are four basic yogas, or paths to union with the Absolute. By far the most popular path within the Hindu tradition is the path of love and devotion, since the easiest way to stir human beings is through the emotions. This is the path of bhakti yoga. Jnana yoga is the path of knowledge and wisdom. Karma yoga is the path of work or service, and raja yoga is a more complex, esoteric path that employs a variety of mind-body techniques. Huston Smith describes raja yoga as "the way to God through psychophysical exercises."[24]

For simplicity's sake, these four paths can be reduced to two, bhakti and jnana. In karma yoga, work or service is either dedicated to the divine or performed simply because it is appropriate or "right," without attachment to specific results. In the former case, the karma yogi is regarded as acting in the spirit of bhakti and in the latter, the spirit of jnana. Raja yoga is said to include all yogic techniques, including control of the body, energy, and mind. Ultimately, however, there must be complete surrender, and this is accomplished either through the heart or the head or, in other words, bhakti or jnana.

The devotional or heart path is by far the most widely practiced since human beings are easily moved by emotions and most especially by the pursuit of love. Most religions contain devotional sects, and the Western religions of Judaism, Christianity, and Islam are almost totally devotional, a quality that powerfully shapes Western (and now global) ideas of what religion should be like. At present, there are nearly 2 billion Christians and 1.2 billion Muslims. These alone account for just over 50 percent of the world's 6 billion people.

In bhakti yoga, the yogi channels the emotional power of love toward god or the divine, thereby diverting attention away from the individual self and its worldly concerns. It is common for the devotee to personalize the divinity, somewhat like an omnipotent lover or friend. The image of God as a lover, for instance, is common in both Christian mysticism and Islamic Sufism.

In many devotional religions, God remains apart, an infinitely higher being who will ultimately judge us, sending us to some kind of heaven or hell. In Hinduism, however, bhakti devotees are reminded that God is inside oneself as well outside and that God is formless as well as formed. *Yoga* means "yoke" and connotes unity with the divine. The ultimate goal of the yogi, therefore, is not only communication and relationship with the divine but also unity. For this, the personal self must be surrendered.

Jnana yoga, the path of knowledge and wisdom, is regarded by many as the steepest but most direct path to unity with the divine. On this path, the yogi studies and observes the workings not only of the "external" world but also of the personal self. The goal of this study goes beyond the mere accumulation of information and knowledge to the process of self-transformation. The yogi begins to accept as a matter of fact—rather than as a theory or belief—that the seeming solidity of the individual separate self is an illusion and that all beings share the same underlying oneness.

Gradually self-identification begins to shift from the personal self, ego, or "I" to spirit, the Absolute, emptiness, or God. As with the bhakti yogi, the personal self must be surrendered.

Some prominent teachers within the Hindu tradition point out that bhakti and jnana are the same in essence. If this is indeed correct, it can then be said that the four yogas in effect condense to just one. One of the greatest modern sages, Sri Ramana Maharshi (1879–1950), advised, "Surrender can take effect only when it is done with full knowledge as to what surrender means. Such knowledge comes after enquiry and reflection and ends invariably in self-surrender. There is no difference between Jnana and absolute surrender to the Lord, that is, in thought, word and deed. To be complete, surrender must be unquestioning; the devotee cannot bargain with the Lord.... The eternal, unbroken, natural state of abiding in the Self is *Jnana*. To abide in the Self, you must love the Self. Since God is verily the Self, love of the Self is the love of God; and that is *Bhakti*. *Jnana* and *Bhakti* are thus one and the same."[25]

Buddhism also recognizes that the twin virtues of compassion and wisdom are necessary for perfection and enlightenment. If one recognizes (through wisdom) that the lives of all beings are interconnected and that they share the same source, then compassion and loving-kindness will automatically arise. As we have seen, the moral component of the Noble Eightfold Path is associated with the virtue of compassion. Nonattachment requires letting go or surrender, which is also the opening of the heart.

In approaching spiritual transcendence, the aspirant faces two fundamental sets of choices. The first is between the heart and the intellect. The second is whether to try to achieve one's goal through intense concentration and willpower, trying to shut out of one's consciousness everything except the chosen object of concentration or, alternatively, letting all the objects of consciousness flow freely through but cutting all identification and attachment to them. Both of these choices can be seen in terms of balancing yin and yang, heart and head, passive and active, open acceptance and discriminating focus.

The early Buddhist popularizer Alan Watts points out that the first stage in our search for god or infinite reality is usually the "religious" one in which the Self or Spirit, still identified with ego, seeks god (itself) as an external object. In the next stage, the Self realizes that it is not ego, and therefore identification with the ego is surrendered. Watts notes that there are two basic ways in which we attempt this process.

The first approach is based on intense concentration through meditation, prayer, mantra, gongan, and the like. The more the chosen object of concentration fills the field of consciousness, the less awareness there is of the ego self and even of the external environment. The gap between subject (ego) and object narrows until the object totally fills the field of consciousness. Watts warns that this process is best undertaken within the supervised confines of a monastery. He adds: "As a rule, the identification of the Self with the object of concentration does not last long. Some internal or external event occurs which suddenly 'shatters' the object, bringing identification to an abrupt close. And in one intense moment of vision the pure consciousness of the Self, without any object of identification left in the field of awareness, knows itself alone and immediately."[26]

Watts thinks the second major approach is more suited to modern lifestyles since it does not entail as much intense concentration and potential volatility as the above approach. He comments that while, like every spiritual exercise,

> it involves a considerable degree of concentration and clear attention, it does not consist in removing all objects and impressions from consciousness save one. On the contrary, it is the ability to retain one's normal and everyday consciousness and at the same time let go of it.... One begins to take an objective view of the stream of thoughts, impressions, feelings and experiences which constantly flow through the mind...whereas consciousness normally

lets itself be carried away by the flow, in this case the important
thing is to watch the flow without being carried away.... When
this has been kept up for some time, it becomes apparent that there
is a ground or inmost centre of consciousness which always watches
and witnesses...this is of course the pure consciousness of the Self
which is never really and principally limited by finite experience.[27]

While Watts claims this latter approach is characteristic of the Chinese
Daoists, I feel it can just as well be a description of vipassana practice.
The modern Tibetan Buddhist master Chogyam Trungpa, like Alan
Watts, pointed that there are two basic types of meditation—the heart
path, which is based on concentration through prayer, and a second path
that aims at the "discovery of the nature of things" and that he associates
with vipassana practice:

It is not the result of some long-term, arduous practice through
which we build ourselves up into a "higher state" nor does it ne-
cessitate going into any kind of inner trance state.... In this kind
of meditation practise the concept of nowness plays a very important part.... One has to become aware of the present moment
through such means as concentrating on the breathing.... If one
cultivates this intelligent intuitive insight, then gradually, stage
by stage, the real intuitive feeling develops and the imaginary or
hallucinatory element is gradually clarified and eventually dies
out.... This is what one tries to achieve through vipassana or
"Insight" meditation.... Reality gradually expands so that we do
not have a technique at all. And in this case one does not have to
concentrate inwards but one can expand outwards more and more.
And the more one expands, the closer one gets to the realisation
of centreless existence.[28]

In summary, when we take an overall look at the elements necessary
for self-transcendence or enlightenment, we can approach through the

head or the heart, and the dynamic of our approach can be doing or non-doing (see diagram). It seems that as we approach realization all elements begin to merge into one.

In comparing Mahayana's Zen and Theravada's vipassana, it would seem reasonable to conclude that their goal is the same and that differences in practice relate to how the practitioner balances the "three essentials" of shila, samadhi, and pañña or prajna.

All this theory brings us back to that dynamic but elusive quality of balance, which is central to Daoism. It must be remembered that the interplay of yin and yang takes place not only between the elements on one plane of consciousness but also between the different levels of consciousness—the physical, emotional, intellectual, and transcendental.

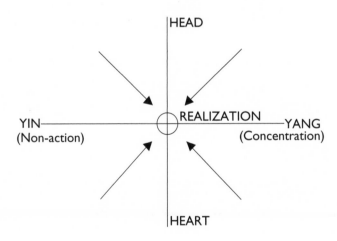

4

Energy, Sex, and Enlightenment

It is important to note that the Shaolin Temple's twin legacies of Chan and the martial arts have been introduced and popularized in the West with a heavy overlay of Japanese culture. Much of this culture was shaped by the seven-hundred-year-long samurai/shogun dominance of Japan, which lasted until the late nineteenth century. The samurai adopted Zen as their religion of choice because of its directness and simplicity and because it enabled them to kill and be killed with equanimity in the service of their overlord. As we shall see, this was very different from the spirit and motivation of the original fighting Shaolin monks.

Having followed Suzuki's advice to look to China to understand the true nature of Chan/Zen, we have so far discovered the powerful and pervasive influence of philosophical Daoism. But other questions remain. Why has the Shaolin Temple's legacy of the martial and mind-body healing arts often been ignored by certain Buddhist scholars? If there is indeed a connection between these two legacies, is it relevant and helpful to the average person today?

The Esoteric Paths of Raja Yoga and Tantra

Perhaps the reasons for this neglect or denial are that these arts are commonly regarded as unconnected with higher spirituality and are relatively esoteric. But that they are esoteric does not mean that they cannot be understood. Some readers might protest that the Chinese martial arts are not esoteric because they are practiced by millions of people all over the world. While this is certainly true, what is popularly practiced is an exercise, sport, or form of self-defense—not many people's practice includes an integrated form of transformational spirituality, that embraces body, qi, and higher mind.

The similarities between raja yoga, some aspects of Tibetan Buddhism, and what the Chinese now call qigong have become increasingly apparent to me over the years. I think it would be helpful to elaborate these characteristics since the connections between these disciplines are not well known or widely acknowledged. Moreover, the practice of tantra, which has weaved its way through much of Hinduism, has also affected Buddhism, especially in Tibet. Since Tibet has long been regarded by the Chinese as part of China, it would not be reckless to speculate that tantric ideas and practices have also had an impact on China. It should indeed be expected.

Huston Smith, we've seen, describes raja yoga as "the way to God through psychophysical exercises." He writes: "Arguing that affairs of the spirit can be approached as empirically as can outer nature, she [India] encourages people who possess the requisite inclination and willpower to seek God in laboratory fashion. The approach calls for a strong suspicion that our true selves are more than we now realize and a passion to plumb their full extent…. [U]nlike most experiments in the natural sciences, those of raja yoga are on one's self, not external nature."[29]

Over a hundred years ago the renowned Hindu sage Swami Vivekananda also described raja yoga as a form of inwardly directed science: "For thousands of years such [extraordinary mental] phenomena have been studied, investigated and generalized; the whole ground of the religious faculties of man have been analysed; and the practical result is Raja-yoga. Raja-yoga does not, after the unpardonable manner of some modern sciences, deny the existence of facts which are difficult to explain…. It declares that each man is only a conduit for the infinite ocean of knowledge and power that lies behind mankind…. There is no supernatural, says the yogi, but there are in nature gross manifestations and subtle manifestations. The subtle are the causes, the gross are the effects. The gross can be easily perceived by the senses; not so the subtle. The practice of raja-yoga will lead to the acquisition of the subtle perceptions."[30]

The process of self-exploration and self-development in raja yoga has eight stages (as does the Buddha's Noble Eightfold Path), or different types of practice. The first two stages are moral in nature as the yogi begins to pay attention to conduct and lifestyle. First come the five *yamas,* or abstentions: injury (of others), lying, stealing, sensuality, and greed. Next are the five *niyamas,* or observances: cleanliness, contentment, self-control, studiousness, and contemplation of the divine.

The third stage is the practice of *asana,* or postures, which regulate the physical body in order to make it fit and healthy. Much of raja yoga's *asana* practice is to be found in today's hatha yoga, which is currently so popular. In terms of spiritual practice, it is important for the body not only to be healthy but also to be able to remain still for long periods of time. This usually requires that the spine be held erect so that the head, neck, and chest are in a straight line. Probably the most famous *asana* is the cross-legged lotus posture, which is used by many spiritual traditions for sitting meditation. Postures may also be standing or reclining.

The fourth step, *pranayama,* is commonly interpreted as breathing exercises but more accurately means the control of *prana,* or vital energy. As we shall see, prana is in many ways similar to the Chinese concept of qi. Swami Vivekananda describes prana as "the infinite, omnipresent manifesting power of this universe…the sum total of all forces in the universe, mental or physical, when resolved back to their original state."[31] He specifically mentions, as manifestations of prana, *akasa* (the omnipresent material of the universe), energy, force, motion, gravitation, magnetism, actions of the body, nerve currents, and "thought-force."

Vivekananda states that mind healers, faith healers, Christian Scientists, hypnotists, and distance healers are all manipulating prana, whether or not they see it in those terms. There is one continuous substance, which links us and makes us one. The mind can exert control over prana, which is not limited by distance. Oneness and interconnectedness occur on all levels—the physical, mental, and the ultimate plane of the Self. The physical plane vibrates relatively slowly. The mind vibrates faster, and Spirit or Self even more so. All, however, is prana.

Pranayama includes the ability not only to control the motions of the lungs but also to sense and balance the prana in the body, both for personal health and to project prana for healing and other purposes.

A special part of pranayama practice, dealing with the control of "psychic" prana, is kundalini yoga. This yoga envisions that within the spine there is a hollow canal called the *sushumna*, which is flanked by two nerve currents called the *pingala* and *ida*. The energy known as *kundalini* is likened to a serpent, coiled at the base of the spine. When awakened and guided by pranayama, this energy ascends the spine, opening and activating various energy centers, or chakras. The highest chakras, located at the top of the head and beyond, are associated with a consciousness that has been variously termed transpersonal, transcendental, and divine.

Within the kundalini tradition it is believed that sexual thoughts and actions, if restrained, can be transformed into a higher form of spiritual energy called *ojas*, which is stored in the brain. Thus, many raja yoga and kundalini teachers feel that celibacy is essential for successful spiritual practice.

The last four stages of raja yoga relate to the mind. *Pratacharya*, the fifth stage, is the withdrawal of the senses, or gathering inward of the mind. The yogi begins to recognize the automatic responses of the mind and the power that unexamined belief exerts over it. Awareness must be increased to prevent the mind from running on uncontrolled. *Dharana,* the sixth step, is concentration of the mind, teaching it to hold on to its object, undistracted.

The seventh step is *dhyana,* or meditation, which as we have seen is the origin of the name Chan and later still Zen. During this stage, concentration deepens and the feeling of separateness vanishes. *Samadhi* is the final, superconscious state, wherein the human being is absorbed in the Absolute. Vivekanada explains, "When one has so intensified the power of dhyana as to be able to reject the external part of perception and meditate only on the internal part, the meaning, that state is called Samadhi.... This meditative state is the highest state of existence. So long as there is desire no real happiness can come. It is only the contemplative, witness-like study of objects that brings us real enjoyment and happiness.... Samadhi is the property of every human being.... Each of the steps to attain samadhi has been reasoned out, properly adjusted and scientifically organized. When faithfully practiced, they will surely lead to the desired end. Then all sorrows cease, all miseries vanish. The seeds of action are burnt, and the Soul will be free forever."[32]

The other major esoteric tradition that has influenced both Hinduism and Buddhism is Tantra or Tantrism. These are terms used to describe an elusive, unconventional, and ritualistic current of spirituality that has woven its way through various Hindu and Buddhist traditions for over fifteen hundred years. The Sanskrit roots of the word *tantra* suggest not only weaving and interpenetration but also extension. The latter is generally taken to mean that tantra practices do not replace the basic spiritual theories and practices with which they have become interwoven, but they are an extension or addition to them.

Common claims within Tantrism are to enlightenment within this lifetime together with worldly well-being. In the tantric view, the practice of spirituality is not incompatible with normal, everyday life. Robert Brown writes:

> Enlightenment, often seen as a difficult process of endless re-
> births achievable only by advanced religious specialists, can be
> reached in Tantrism during one lifetime while the practitioner is
> still alive. On the other hand, worldly power, even of the most
> mundane kind, for example success in love, is also achievable at
> the same time as enlightenment; they are intertwined. Success in
> this world need not be shunned to achieve enlightenment, a po-
> sition held by *sramanic* [mendicant] Buddhists, Jains and the
> Brahmanic tradition of the Hindus. For non-Tantric Buddhists,
> Jains and Hindus, the life of a householder is a serious impediment
> for full spiritual accomplishment.[33]

Instead of forcing its adherents to choose between God and sex, tantra teaches that it is possible to harness the tremendous power of sexual energy for the purposes of spiritual transformation. Under the guidance and supervision of a qualified guru, adherents channel the feelings of love and ecstasy generated by sexual union into egolessness. In addition to this bhakti-like practice, tantra also commonly uses the kundalini practices of raja yoga, whereby the shakti or kundalini energy, instead of being expended in the ejaculation of sperm, is led up the spine through the various chakras to the brain. This is seen as a way of tapping into and utilizing the boundless energy that flows throughout the universe.

Tantra often has elaborate rituals, which are also used to try to control universal energy. Andre Padoux writes,

> The ideological aspect of the tantric vision is the cosmos as per-
> meated by power (or powers), a vision wherein energy *(sakti)* is
> both cosmic and human and where microcosm and macrocosm

correspond and interact. The ideology is important because it
explains such tantric features as the concept and practice of *kundalini,* as well as a number of yogic and ritual practices for the
use and control of that power. It also explains some aspects of the
speculations and practices concerning the power of the word *(vac),*
especially the nature and power of mantras. This ideology not
only colors, but orientates and organizes, and gives meaning to
all tantric practices and observances.[34]

In tantra the whole body is employed as a tool in religious practices.
Sounds *(mantras),* visual objects *(mandalas),* and hand gestures *(mudras)*
are commonly used. Mandalas are ritual or sacred diagrams representing
different aspects of everyday life, of the Dharma and of divinity. They can
be created in sand, on paper, and through hand gestures. Within Tibetan
Buddhism, the visualization of deities (deity yoga) is used for generating
what Jeffrey Hopkins calls "calm abiding and special insight." Hopkins
cautions:

> It is important to recognize clearly that the special features of
> tantra are in addition to the bodhisattva ideals; thus any discus-
> sion of using sexual desire and so forth in tantra is neither con-
> trary to nor a substitute for the wish to achieve others' happiness,
> even if the terms "compassion" and "mind of enlightenment" are
> sometimes used to refer to bliss and essential bodily fluids. Rather
> it is a means of allowing certain highly qualified people to achieve
> altruistic buddhahood more quickly than would otherwise be pos-
> sible, by utilizing the subtler, blissful consciousness associated
> with sexual union and so forth to realize emptiness.[35]

Chogyam Trungpa, in *Cutting through Spiritual Materialism,* empha-
sizes the importance of the energy aspect of tantra and of samsara, or the
everyday world, to our spiritual transformation:

While the basic teaching of Mahayana Buddhism is concerned
with developing *prajna,* transcendental knowledge, the basic
teaching of tantra is connected with working with energy. Energy
is described in the *Kriyayoga Tantra of Vajramala* as "that which
abides in the heart of all beings, self-existing simplicity, that which
sustains wisdom. This indestructible essence is the energy of great
joy; it is all-pervasive, like space. This is the dharma body of non-
dwelling.".... Tantric wisdom brings *nirvana* into *samsara.*....The
term "ordinary wisdom," *thamal-gyi-shepa,* is used a great deal in
the tantric tradition. It is the completely ordinary version of "form
is form, emptiness is empty"; it is what is. One cannot reject the
physical existence of the world as being something bad and associated with *samsara.* You can only understand the essence of *nirvana* by looking into the essence of *samsara.*[36]

Nagaboshi Tomio (Terence Dukes) makes an ambitious attempt in
his book *The Bodhisattva Warriors* to establish direct, specific, and comprehensive links between the Vajramukti martial arts of the Indian warrior class (the Ksatriyas), the Chinese martial arts originating from the
Shaolin Temple, and Tibetan Vajrayana Buddhism.

Dukes points out that the Buddha, as a Ksatriya prince, underwent
Vajramukti training, which included patterned training sequences of attack and defense called *nata.* He speculates that the Buddhists in Northern
India over time adopted this fighting system, adding spiritual, healing,
and eventually tantric elements to it, terming their practice "Bodhisattva
Vajramukti." He states that although the word *nata* in India is now usually associated with dance and mime movements, it originally referred to
fighting postures, which in turn evolved into tantric mudras. Dukes claims
that these nata/mudras are the basis of many of the classical Chinese
fighting postures, especially those that are associated with the Shaolin
Temple.

Dukes attaches great significance to the name *Vajramukti*, which he translates as "Thunderbolt Fist." He claims that Bodhisattva Vajramukti was passed on within the confines of Chinese Buddhist temples and became known to the Chinese as *chuan fa*. Dukes argues that *chuan fa* should be translated as "closed hand of the Dharma," with *chuan* meaning "closed hand" and *fa* meaning "Dharma." He thinks "closed hand" intimates a secret or esoteric doctrine. The Chinese normally translate *chuan* as "fist" and *fa* as "method" or "system."

Dukes writes that Bodhisattva Vajramukti was "a powerful and potentially dangerous cathartic physical practice. Because it dealt directly with the liberation and channeling of primitive energies and instincts within mankind, a teacher powerful in both body and mind was necessary to convey its principles and guide its students,"[37] Closed-door instruction was given only to carefully selected students. Dukes states that schools that dealt with such energies were called by the Buddhists *Vajrayana* or "Thunderbolt Path" and were introduced into Tibet during the eighth century C.E. Dukes also claims that these esoteric lineages later reached Okinawa and Japan.

While *The Bodhisattva Warriors* contains much fascinating and useful information and its general theories seem plausible, Dukes is given to arbitrary conclusions and judgments, many of these critical of the Chinese contribution to chuan fa. This is a strange stance to take, since almost all the modern Asian martial arts are traceable to China (not India) and most extant historical records are also of Chinese origin. Dukes admits that because so many historical records (along with temples and their inhabitants) in Northern India were destroyed during nearly eight centuries of devastating Muslim raids and invasions, much of his book is speculation and "much of what we know concerning *nata* within Indian Buddhism comes to us via Chinese tradition and Buddhist writing."[38]

Dukes summarily dismisses the many legends and records of patriotic Shaolin fighting monks, speculating, "It was probably these same secular people—often political refugees or fugitives from justice or debt—who later comprised the monastic 'armies' said to have fought in pitched battles for various Emperors."[39] He, however, admits to the existence in China of *Dharmapalas*, "warrior-trained monks whose duty it was to guard the holy relics, the treasures of shrines and occasionally teachers of the Dharma from robbers…. [S]uch protectors were not only active in this physical realm, but also in other dimensions of being."[40]

Dukes is particularly negative with regard to Daoists. The index of *The Bodhisattva Warriors* contains just three references to Taoism in nearly five hundred pages. One is a single-line mention and the other two are sweepingly uncomplimentary. The first one reads: "Taoism was only organized and systematized in the first and second centuries a.d. (perhaps as a result of the introduction of Buddhism and a consequent fear on the part of the Taoist elite that its sources of power and finance might be threatened)."[41] And the second: "Newly developing Taoism also plagiarized *Chuan Fa*'s physical techniques and, ignoring its spirituality, created 'new' systems of their own martial arts. By such surreptitious and presumptuous methods, non-Buddhists came to learn *Chuan Fa* techniques bereft of their spiritual teachings, and cursed successive generations by popularizing this travesty."[42]

As regards the development of medicine in China, Dukes opines: "Unfortunately the early Taoist healers and magicians hijacked many of these real discoveries and for several centuries proceeded to add or overlay them with various metaphysical and idiosyncratic doctrines. As a result, the development of useful healing techniques was slowed for several centuries. Such retardation was not restricted to medicine alone but spread to many other parts of Chinese society."[43]

Dukes's book has stirred controversy not only because of his novel theories but also because some of his own lineage claims, mainly Tibetan and Japanese, have been disputed. The more conventional view is that ever since distant antiquity there have been similarities between the cultures and beliefs of India and China and that when Buddhism entered China it had a significant, enduring, and mostly positive effect on the Chinese. It is generally accepted that China in turn influenced Buddhism through its contributions to the development of both the Mahayana and Vajrayana branches of Buddhism.

For all practical purposes, Chan Buddhism was the result of the coming together of the Chinese and Indian cultures, regardless of the precise mix or proportion of their respective influences. Even as eminent an authority on Zen as D.T. Suzuki did not care to go back to India to dig up the earlier roots of Chan because it did not matter. Chan is important because it can help us here and now, and because it is always about the ongoing transformation of consciousness. Speculation aside, neither Chan nor chuan fa existed in India as far as we know.

Similarly, if the Chan and martial/esoteric lineages of Shaolin are indeed linked, then one of the most important questions we must ask is how this affects our current understanding and practice of Chan and of transformative spirituality in general.

Qigong: Medical, Martial, and Spiritual

Present-day Shaolin monks still practice both Chan Buddhism and martial arts, of which qigong is an important part. They credit qigong with giving them extraordinary abilities, beyond mere physical training. Shaolin legend has it that when Bodhidharma found the monks at Shaolin Temple too sickly to meditate, he taught them health-giving exercises, which are generally regarded to have been qigong. In China, over the millennia, qigong has been used for three interrelated purposes: health and healing, martial arts, and spiritual transformation. Legend tells us that all three for a long time have been practiced in an integrated manner at the Shaolin Temple.

Qi, as we have seen, means universal life energy, vital energy, breath, gas, air, or ether. *Gong* means skill or benefit derived from persistent work or practice over time. Thus the meaning of "qigong" as "expertise regarding qi" is fairly close to that of raja yoga's *pranayama*.

Qi was a part of Chinese culture long before Bodhidharma and even before the entry of Buddhism into China. Qi had been mentioned in China's earliest literary treasures like the *Yi Jing,* the seminal Daoist works of Laozi and Zhuangzi, and of course the Yellow Emperor's Classic of Internal Medicine. The early Chinese image of the sage was of one who lived in harmony with the Dao, conserving qi through a moderate lifestyle and nourishing it through regulation of the mind, breath, and posture. The Yellow Emperor's Classic states that if the sage is "tranquilly content in nothingness," then his or her qi and spirit will be preserved, preventing any illness. Zhuangzi talks about listening not with the *mind* but with a qi that is empty and therefore receptive.

In addition to a quiet mind, the Chinese saw great benefit in using breathing techniques, coordinated with movement, to lead and guide the qi. These early forms of qigong were often called *dao yin,* which in this context means "to lead and guide the qi." Some dao yin movements were based on the observation of various animals, birds, or reptiles. Zhuangzi for instance, recommended moving like a bear and stretching like a bird. *The Spring and Autumn Annals,* one of ancient China's Six Classics, mentions certain dances that were used to guide the breath in order to relieve congestion and stagnation of energy. A piece of silk recovered in 1973 from the tomb of King Ma (second century B.C.E.) shows forty-four dao yin postures—some with animal names, some associated with specific ailments—which remarkably seem to cover much of modern qigong practice. The most famous dao yin exercises based on animal movements were the Five Animal Frolics *(wu qin xi)* created by the great physician Hua Tuo (110–207 C.E.) These graceful exercises imitated the movements of the crane, bear, monkey, deer, and tiger.

From ancient times the Chinese also developed the notion that the martial arts, wushu, quite apart from their military or self-defense applications, could be beneficial for health and overall development or "cultivation of virtue." No less an authority than China's "First Teacher," Confucius, had recommended training in both the literary arts and martial arts to bring about a more balanced, rounded person. In *The Spring and Autumn of Chinese Martial Arts* Kang Gewu writes:

> The concept of holistic Wushu appeared as early as the Spring and Autumn, and the Warring States Period. Yue Nu, a female sword specialist in the Yue Kingdom, talked about sword play which already consisted of the concept of unity in external and internal exercises and the shaping of *Qi* and spirit etc. Later Wushu practitioners, making use of the concept of "integration between Heaven and Human Beings" put forward by the Han Dynasty Confucianists, perfected the concept of holistic Wushu. They regard Nature as a large universe and the human body as a small universe within the large one. Between Nature and Human Beings exists an interactive relationship which requires unification of the movements of people and Heaven (Nature). The human body's internal consciousness, breathing and force must be unified with external positions."[44]

Yue Nu is dated about 500 B.C.E. The Han dynasty ruled from 202 B.C.E. to 220 C.E.

As wushu became part of the Chinese cultural landscape, other aspects developed. During the Warring States Period (throughout the third century B.C.E.), wushu became established as a popular form of entertainment called *jiao di* (wrestling play), which later incorporated acrobatics. Some wushu styles began to mimic the spirit and movements of animals, especially after Hua Tuo's Five Animal Frolics. These styles were called *xiang xing quan* (imitation boxing). There also began to circulate the idea that a true martial arts master should also be a healer—to be able to repair any damages and, better still, prevent conflict altogether.

All the diverse seeds of Chinese culture came together and blossomed during the Tang dynasty (618–907 C.E.), which is widely regarded as a period of unparalleled excellence in arts, science, and technology. Many scholars including Joseph Campbell think that Buddhism, which became China's official religion, played an important part in this blossoming. Campbell writes of the Tang dynasty that "the first part of this richly cosmopolitan period saw the flowering, but the second part the shattering, of the Buddhist Order in China. Ch'an, the sect of silence, held the lead in the work of Sinicizing the doctrine."[45]

Buddhism sparked a revival in both Confucianism and especially Daoism. Religious Daoism (in contrast to philosophical and esoteric Daoism) arose in response to Buddhism, borrowing many of its rituals, ideas, and structures. The Chinese generally became much more interested in metaphysical matters and especially in the nature and functioning of qi.

Starting around the ninth century C.E., during the latter part of the Tang dynasty, philosophers and thinkers started consciously combining elements from all of China's "three doctrines" of Confucianism, Daoism, and Buddhism. These newly fashioned doctrines were called *dao xue,* which literally means "study of the Dao," but have become known in English somewhat awkwardly as "Neo-Confucianism." One of the best-known and most influential Neo-Confucian philosophers was Zhou Dun-Yi (1017–73), creator of the famous tai chi diagram (*taiji tu,* the yin-yang symbol) and its accompanying commentary, which was based on his study of the "appendices" of the *Yi Jing.* The comprehensive Daoist canon, containing 1,120 works, was compiled not long afterward, during the twelfth century.

The Tang dynasty inventions of printing and gunpowder (both invented in China centuries before they appeared in Europe) greatly contributed to this intermingling process—the former by spreading ideas much more rapidly and accurately and the latter by shifting the emphasis in wushu practice. In addition to *troop* or *battle wushu, folk wushu* developed rapidly. The latter included *show wushu (hua fa wuyi)* for entertainment, which became more elaborate and was incorporated into poetic drama accompanied by music. Folk wushu developed three different kinds of practice: *tao lu*, which were patterns or routines of movement, *gong fa*, which were methods for practice of special skills *(gong)*, and *ge dou*, which were fighting or combat methods.

All of these developments and intermixtures helped produce the art and practice we currently know as qigong. Although it is still common to classify qigong as either Buddhist, Daoist, or Confucian qigong, and its applications as either martial, medical, or spiritual, none of these classifications is totally accurate, for they are all interrelated, both philosophically and practically. Thus, in a broad sense, we can say that modern qigong is one of the (largely unacknowledged) prominent offspring of Buddhism's marriage with the native Chinese culture and as such is relevant to the understanding and practice of Chan, a uniquely Chinese form of Buddhism.

The acceptance of qi as a reality is of course central to qigong. Fung Yu-lan writes that the Neo-Confucianists regarded qi in its more abstract sense as the "primary undifferentiated material out of which all individual things are formed" and in its more concrete or denser sense as physical matter. Kristofer Schipper states that at the beginning of "Heaven and Earth," qi is pure but as yet undifferentiated energy-matter in the matrix of primordial chaos. "At a given point the matrix comes to maturity, breaks up and frees the *ch'i* (breaths, energies) contained within which then escape and separate. The light, transparent *ch'i* rise and form heaven; the heavy opaque ones sink, forming Earth. Thus having established the polarity of Heaven and Earth, the *ch'i* join and unite in the Center, which constitutes a third fundamental modality. The Three complete each other, forming composite entities, 'The Ten Thousand Beings.'"[46]

The Chinese did not stop with the generalization that everything is qi, which would not have been of much practical use, but went on to theorize that qi moves in specific ways that can be observed not only within human beings but also in the terrestrial environment and the sun, moon, and stars. The study of qi within humans is qigong; within the heavens, it is astrology; and within the earth, it is known as *feng shui*, literally "wind-water." Of course since everything is qi, heaven, earth, and the human are all interconnected and affect each other.

The Chinese, like the Indians, very early on tested their theories of energy in the field of medicine. Acupuncture is perhaps the most famous branch of traditional Chinese medicine, but there are other branches: herbalism, massage, and medical qigong. All four branches use the same theories for diagnosis but employ different methods of treatment.

Although Chinese medicine is based on the seemingly unscientific notions of qi and yin-yang theory, its reputation for efficacy is gaining many converts, even within the conventional, Western medical establishment. Since the 1950s, numerous Western-style studies have been conducted, especially in China, on all aspects of traditional Chinese medicine including qigong. They generally have come to the same conclusion that the ordinary Chinese have known for hundreds of years: it works. In *The Way of Qigong,* Kenneth Cohen explains qigong in terms of Western medicine and describes several studies in detail. Ted Kaptchuk does the same for traditional Chinese medicine in general and describes attempts to isolate certain elements of Chinese medicine in order to incorporate them into the framework of modern western medicine. He concludes:

> Fortunately for its future, however, the results of the studies generally demonstrate that traditional Chinese medicine does work best when left in the context of Chinese logic. In most cases, pattern weaving based on Yin-Yang theory produced better clinical results than the mechanical application of Chinese remedies within a Western context.... This is because the Chinese view of health and disease as inseparable from a specific person means the treatment will be well tailored to that person. Such personal

shaping seems to maximize the effectiveness of the therapies. Western clinical studies of traditional Chinese medicine, by proving its practical efficacy, have helped it win its battle for survival in the twentieth century and promise it a place in the future of medicine.[47]

Yin-Yang and the Five Elements

At this juncture, it seems pertinent to examine yin-yang theory in more detail, since it is the basis of traditional Chinese medicine, much of qigong practice, and, as we shall see in the next chapter, the Daoist "internal" martial arts.

In China, the concept and study of qi is inextricably linked with the classical theories of yin-yang and the Five Elements. Zhou Dun-Yi, the Neo-Confucian philosopher, in his explanation of the famous yin-yang symbol, or tai chi diagram *(taiji tu)*, stated:

> The Supreme Ultimate through movement produces *Yang*. This movement having reached its limit, is followed by quiescence and by this quiescence, it produces the *Yin*. When quiescence has reached its limit, there is a return to movement. Thus movement and quiescence in alternation become each the source of the other. The distinction between *Yin* and *Yang* is determined and these Two Forms [*Yin* and *Yang*] stand revealed. By transformations of the *Yang* and the union therewith of *Yin*, Water, Fire, Wood, Metal and Soil are produced. These Five Ethers [ch'i, i.e., Elements] become diffused in harmonious order and the four seasons proceed in their course. The Five Elements are the one *Yin* and *Yang*; the *Yin* and *Yang* are the one Supreme Ultimate; and the Supreme Ultimate is fundamentally the Ultimateless.[48]

Giovanni Maciocia, in his widely used text of traditional Chinese medicine, *The Foundations of Chinese Medicine*, writes:

The Concept of Yin-Yang is probably the single most important and distinctive theory of Chinese Medicine. It could be said that all Chinese medical physiology, pathology and treatment can, eventually, be reduced to Yin-Yang. The concept of Yin-Yang is extremely simple, yet very profound. One can seemingly understand it on a rational level, and yet continually find new expressions of it in clinical practice and indeed, in life. The concept of Yin-Yang, together with that of *Qi,* has permeated Chinese philosophy over the centuries and is radically different to any Western philosophical idea…. Yin and Yang represent opposite but complementary qualities. Each thing or phenomenon could be itself and its contrary. [49]

In contrast to the Western idea of mutually exclusive opposites, yin and yang are complementary and interdependent. Each contains a seed of the other and can transform into the other under various circumstances. These principles are applied in very specific ways in traditional Chinese medicine. By way of simple example, if you are invaded by external cold (yin), from the weather, air-conditioners, or the like, and it remains trapped in the body, it will turn to heat (yang), which you will feel as fever. Or again, if the "water" energy (yin) in the body is not sufficient to balance the "fire" element (yang), the latter will get out of control and manifest heat signs— headaches, red eyes and face, dry skin, and thirst.

Although the yin-yang symbol or diagram has become somewhat of a pop culture cliché, it is still widely misunderstood. In particular, many people do not seem to realize that one easily transforms into the other, that the yin-yang dynamic is taking place at several different levels of consciousness or functioning, and that underlying the interplay of yin and yang *(taiji)* is emptiness *(wuji).* This means that there is unity underlying diversity and stillness underlying activity. We cannot experience this, however, if we hold on to and identify with the particular, as, for example, we justify stereotypical gender behavior by simplistic assertions of inherent differences.

If we look around our everyday lives, there is very little evidence of yin-yang philosophy being understood, let alone being put into practice. Our leaders, seemingly ignorant of history, still talk in terms of the ultimate victory of "good" over "evil" and promise they will go to any lengths to achieve it. This win-at-any-cost attitude is also prevalent in business, entertainment, and sport, which among them provide almost all popular role models. Many women, instead of exploring their own natural strengths, seek power by aping men even to the extent of grotesque body shaping. Our leaders argue (seemingly successfully) that the poor will benefit if the rich get richer. We seek unity by emphasizing competition and separateness. We continually try to defeat or tame nature with science and technology, forgetting that we ourselves are part of nature. Indeed, we treat our own bodies in this fashion. Much of the widespread alienation, separation, stress, conflict, and disease we experience would not arise if we understood and followed yin-yang philosophy. We do not need greater material resources or more advanced technology to accomplish this, just some quiet introspection and self-inquiry.

The Five Elements, or Five Phases *(wu xing)*, theory originally existed independently alongside yin-yang theory. Around the fourth century B.C.E., however, attempts were made, especially by the yin-yang, or naturalist, school, to fit the former into the framework of the much older yin-yang theory. As a consequence, the Five Elements or Phases were seen as elaboration of yin-yang dynamics. Kaptchuk writes:

> The theory of Phases is a system of correspondences and patterns
> that subsume events and things, especially in relation to their dy-
> namics.... Wood is associated with active functions that are in a
> growing phase. Fire designates functions that have reached a max-
> imal state of activity and are about to begin a decline or a resting

90 *The Spiritual Legacy of Shaolin Temple*

period. Metal represents functions in a declining state. Water represents functions that have reached a maximal state of rest and are about to change the direction of their activity. Finally, Earth designates balance or neutrality. In a sense Earth is a buffer between the other Phases.[50]

The Chinese sought to identify Five Phases correspondences in the natural world just as they had done with yin-yang correspondences. For example, wood-fire-earth-metal-water correspondences were seen in terms of directions (east-south-center-west-north), yin bodily organs (liver-heart-spleen-lungs-kidney), emotions (anger-joy-worry-grief-fear), colors (green-red-yellow-white-dark blue), tastes (sour-bitter-sweet-pungent-salty) and seasons (spring-summer-neutral/transition-autumn-winter), to mention but a few.

There are various cycles, or sequences, that operate between the elements, or phases. The "generating," or production, cycle is the most common way of listing the elements: wood generates fire, which generates earth, which generates metal, which generates water, which generates wood. The element that generates or produces is regarded as the (nourishing) mother or parent, while the element generated is seen as the child (which in turn becomes a mother). In the "controlling," or checking, sequence, wood controls earth, earth controls water, water controls fire, fire controls metal, and metal controls wood.

As an example of how a traditional doctor might use the Five Phases theory in clinical practice, we can imagine that after interviewing, observing, and taking the pulse of a patient, the doctor concludes that the patient's liver qi is deficient. Although the doctor can simply try to increase or "tonify" the liver qi, it would be wise to inquire into why the deficient condition occurred. Using the Five Element theory, one avenue of inquiry would be to check whether the "mother" organ, in this case the kidneys, is itself deficient and therefore not strong enough to nourish the "child." An alternative is that perhaps the liver is being over controlled by the lungs, which is associated with grief. Perhaps the liver's child, the heart, is too fired up with emotion and is draining its mother. Further questioning of the patient concerning relationships and lifestyle may strongly point toward one or more of the possible causes.

The Five Phases theory has been criticized as arbitrary, illogical, and impractical almost since it was put forward over two thousand years ago. Many modern doctors who practice traditional Chinese medicine, however, still use it to elaborate on or double-check their conclusions first reached through yin-yang theory. They find it useful; it works for them and their patients.

The Three Regulations of Qigong

Although qigong can lead to seemingly extraordinary abilities, it is actually natural: we all have qi and are manifestations of qi. If we understand how qi works, then it would be natural to use it to enhance our lives and endeavors, akin to learning how to read and write.

Qigong's applications are innumerable; the whole universe is qi. The Chinese see the human as the connection between heaven and earth and therefore always influenced by heaven qi and earth qi. The Three Treasures of the heavens are the sun, moon, and stars; and of the earth, wind, water, and earth. In an agricultural society like ancient China, the importance of all these factors would have been obvious, but even in a modern urban city people are affected by them, although they remain largely unaware of the connection: women's menstrual cycles, erratic behavior associated with a full moon, tides, solar storms, storms, floods, earthquakes. Energy and people flow through a house in a similar manner to wind and water. Each of us can directly observe this fact if we so choose.

In Daoist and medical qigong, human beings also have Three Treasures—*jing* (essence), *qi* (energy), and *shen* (spirit). Qigong developed Three Regulations to work with these Three Treasures—regulation of posture, breathing, and mind respectively. Since the Three Treasures are all interrelated, however, each of the regulations affects all Three Treasures.

Jing is the densest of the Three Treasures, with the slowest rate of vibration. It is our basic life essence, sustaining the physical body and forming the basis of our reproductive essence. The prenatal or innate part of our jing is inherited from our parents and determines our physical constitution. This type of jing diminishes as we get older, since it is used up in facilitating the transformation of postnatal jing and qi, which is acquired from food and air, and in producing reproductive essence—ova in women and sperm in men. Hans Selye, in speaking of what he called "the stress syndrome," used as part of his theory the notion that each person is born with a finite supply of "adaptation energy," which is uncannily similar to the concept in traditional Chinese medicine of inherited, "pre-heaven" qi and essence.

In qigong, jing is gathered and transformed into qi in the lower *dantian* (energy center or "elixir field"), which is located below the navel. This is the same area that the Japanese call the *hara*. Many Oriental paintings and statues show bodhisattvas, monks, and warriors with pronounced bellies, which contrast with the current Western ideal of beauty and strength. These bellies do not indicate fat from overindulgence; rather, they signify ample reservoirs of jing and qi, accumulated through skillful practice of qigong.

Qi, the second of the Three Treasures, interacts with both jing and shen, supporting them and linking them through energetic transference. Qi is the force behind the performance of all activity and is present not only in the human body but throughout the cosmos. Within the human being, qi transforms, transports, protects, sustains, and facilitates. It is perhaps a major component of the "missing link" between mind and body, which Western medicine has so long denied and is now beginning to probe. Candace Pert, a professor and researcher in neuroscience, states, in an interview with Bill Moyers:

> We have sufficient scientific evidence to hypothesize that these in-
> formation molecules, these peptides and receptors, are the bio-
> chemicals of emotions.... Emotions are in two realms. They can
> be in the physical realm, where we're talking about molecules
> whose molecular weight I can tell you and whose sequences I can
> write as formulas. And there's another realm that we experience
> that's not under the purview of science. There are aspects of mind
> that have qualities that seem to be outside of matter.... I person-
> ally think there are many phenomena that we can't explain with-
> out going into energy. As a scientist, I believe that we're going to
> understand everything one day, but this understanding will re-
> quire bringing in a realm we don't understand at all yet.... We're
> going to have to bring in that extra-energy realm, the realm of
> spirit and soul that Descartes kicked out of Western scientific
> thought.[51]

In qigong, qi is associated in particular with the breath and the emotions and is regarded as a form of energy that is subtler than jing. Qi is
transformed into shen within the middle dantian, which is located in the
chest area.

Shen is our spirit, in the sense of a flame of the divine and also of the
consciousness that guides us with intelligence and light. If the shen is
strong and properly housed in the heart, then all other human systems
will tend to be harmonious and in good working order. Jerry Alan Johnson
explains that in qigong there is a difference between the prenatal spirit
(yuan shen) and postnatal spirit *(zhi shen)*:

> Yuan Shen is the body's spiritual element derived from prenatal
> Jing *(yuan jing)* and prenatal Qi *(yuan qi)*.... This aspect of the
> body's Shen is considered to be the intuitive Mind of the Dao.
> It is unborn and undying.... Postnatal Spirit *(zhi shen)* is the spir-
> itual element derived from postnatal Jing and postnatal Qi. This

aspect of the body's Shen is considered to be the conditioned
mind or will, also known as discriminating or acquired mind....
Prenatal and postnatal Shen usually interact intermittently with
each other in maintaining the body's health.[52]

Shen is developed from jing and qi in the upper dantian, which is located at the level of the third eye, and is transformed into wuji (infinite
space or void). This process is likened to steam or smoke dissipating into
space. In turn, wuji returns to the Dao, or the divine. Prolonged emotional
disturbances can weaken the shen, while tranquil qigong or meditation
strengthens it. When energized, shen flows upward like fire and transforms into wuji. A strong shen shines brightly like a light in the eyes and
is capable of leading qi to an injured area for the purpose of healing.

Before we briefly look at how the Three Regulations work, it should
be emphasized that all are necessary because they support each other. For
example, even though shen is considered the highest, that is, most refined
and spiritual, of the Three Treasures, a weak jing and or constant emotional turbulence will hamper efforts to develop it, or even make development impossible. Most efforts at self-improvement tend to focus on just
one aspect—the physical body, energetic and psychic abilities, or the "spiritual" mind. In qigong, all are developed because they are inseparable. A
sound body or strong psychic abilities are not much use if ruled by an erratic mind and unstable emotions.

To an onlooker, qigong self-regulation might appear a puzzling mix-
ture, because regulation of the posture, or postural dao yin, may be either
static or moving. The main static postures are lying, sitting, and standing. Moving postures include walking, yoga-like stretching, and taijiquan-
like movements. Qigong also includes self-massage, gathering energy
from the external environment (plants, trees, rivers, oceans, sun, moon,
stars, etc.), and sound vibration, which is similar to chanting. These "healing sounds" will be discussed as part of respiratory dao yin below.

One of the most important physical postures used in qigong, taiji-quan, and the other internal martial arts is the basic wuji (emptiness) standing posture. This posture aligns the body while facilitating relaxation, breathing, and the proper balance and circulation of qi. Its principles can also be applied in walking, sitting, and other activities such as manual work, sports, and working at a desk. In my personal experience, learning the principles of wuji posture enhanced my existing practice of Buddhist sitting, standing, and walking meditation. A detailed description of the wuji posture is included in chapter 7.

A very popular form of dynamic postural dao yin is walking. It is used for treating diseases of the five yin organs, and in China is widely practiced by cancer patients. An important element of qigong walking therapy is "toe-raised stepping," which touches the heel down first with the toes in an upward position and then lets the foot roll flat in a wavelike motion, pumping the *yongquan* ("bubbling well" point, just inside the ball of the foot). This stepping is especially effective for the meridians of the yin organs that originate in the feet, namely the kidney, spleen, and liver. Although it is common to dismiss qigong walking as just ordinary walking, it must be noted that most people do not walk efficiently for simple body alignment, let alone qigong. If your step (the way your foot makes contact with the ground) is not correct, it can become a chronic and debilitating problem, eventually affecting your ankles, knees, hips, and spine.

Basic walking therapy can be performed at various speeds and may be enhanced with various kinds of breathing, hand swinging, waist rotation, visualization of colors, and so forth, depending on the specific condition of the patient or exerciser.

Dao yin regulation of the body has, from very early times, included self-massage. We can disperse areas of excess and blocked energy or stimulate and tonify deficient ones by using a variety of techniques including rubbing, pressing, slapping, and drumming with the fingertips. These self-massage techniques, known as *an mo,* are generally based on the traditional medical theories of qi flow, meridians, and acupressure points and can therefore be enhanced by intent *(yi),* which guides the qi.

Diet is an important form of body regulation and is considered by the Chinese to be part of herbal medicine. All foods have yin-yang properties, so it is possible (and recommended) to customize your diet according to your own constitution, the region in which you live, and the changing seasons and climate. Much Chinese (and subsequently Japanese and Korean) cuisine is based on general yin-yang principles. The quality of food ingredients is also important, and therefore, in our present environment, this would lead us towards natural, "organic" foods, free of preservatives, insecticides, additives, hormones, genetic modification, and the like…. For example, the ubiquitous soy sauce traditionally was made from fermented soybeans, but instead it now commonly includes preservatives, coloring, salt, and other ingredients combined to mimic the taste. In addition, modern agricultural methods for growing soybeans commonly utilize chemical pesticides and fertilizers as well as genetically modified strains.

The second major type of qigong regulation is regulation of breathing, or respiratory qigong/dao yin. As in Indian hatha and pranayama yoga, the breath is seen as closely linked with our internal energies and has specific effects on the mind (especially on mood, emotions, and altered states of consciousness) and on physiological functions like blood pressure, pulse, and the nervous system. We are becoming more aware that deep breathing is a calming force, but there are several different ways of breathing, which have different effects. In stressful situations, for example, we commonly tense our bodies and hold our breath, but this can result in long-term emotional suppression and body armoring. Increasingly, Western stress-reduction techniques and athletic training are based on breathing techniques that have been taken from yoga or qigong—often out of context. Although such techniques are useful, most people do not realize that their context (which is an integral spirituality) is much more important.

Deep abdominal breathing is fundamental in qigong and can be "natural" or "reverse." In natural breathing, the abdomen expands during inhalation and contracts during exhalation. In reverse breathing, the abdomen, along with the anus and pelvic floor, contract during inhalation, while the qi is often guided up the back; during exhalation, the abdomen relaxes and expands. Other breathing methods include forceful exhalation, holding the breath in the abdomen, and rapid inhalation and exhalation.

The breath, together with visualization, can be used to guide qi around the body for a wide variety of purposes. This is as much mental as respiratory dao yin. One of the best-known practices is the Microcosmic Orbit, or Small Heaven Cycle, whereby the breath and energy are guided from the lower dantian up the spine, over the top of the head, and down the front of the body, back to the lower dantian. This is one of the main energy circuits in the body, and it is important that it be connected and free flowing, since it functions somewhat like a reservoir for the subsidiary meridians and channels. If there is too much energy in the regular meridians, it overflows into the complex of extraordinary meridians, which includes the Microcosmic Orbit. Conversely, if the general level of energy is low in the regular meridians, energy flows from the extraordinary meridians.

The circulation of qi is not confined within the boundaries of the physical body but can be projected into or collected from the external environment. For example, qi may be gathered from the sun, moon, stars, trees, bushes, flowers, ocean, lakes, streams, and so on. In gathering qi from the environment, some qigong practitioners make use of complex rules (mostly based on yin-yang and Five Elements theories) concerning colors, directions, and times of day, month, and year. One of the simplest and most important rules for beginners is to ensure that the environment in which you are gathering is clean and healthy—no pollution, cemeteries, sickly or dying trees, garbage dumps, and the like. The other necessity is an open mind, since in qigong the yi, or intention, directs the qi.

Recently, during a brilliant full moon in a clear sky, which is ideal for collecting moon qi, I invited my seventeen-year-old daughter, Hana, to join me in collecting moon qi. Although she does not practice qigong, the idea of qi is familiar to her. At the end of our brief exercise, which I explained as we went along, I asked her how she felt. She said she felt energized but had suddenly started shivering from the coldness of the energy (even though it was a warm night). Although I had never told her so, moon energy is generally regarded as cold.

Sounds and vibration are also regarded as part of respiratory yao yin and date back to at least the Qin dynasty (221–207 B.C.E.). Early physicians noted that all human beings tend to make the same types of sounds in certain life situations, and eventually specific sounds and vibrations were matched with specific organs according to the Five Elements theory. For example, the sound *ha* (laughing/joy) was identified with the yin organ associated with fire element, the heart, while a sighing or hissing sound was associated with the metal element, the lungs, which store grief.

Probably the most widely practiced healing sounds today are the Six Healing Sounds, which include a sound for each of the five yin organs plus an extra sound for the "Triple Burners," which in traditional Chinese medicine is a notional sixth organ related to the overall functioning of the yang organs. These sounds are used for general regulation, while more specialized "cancer and tumor tone resonations" are used for serious conditions involving growths, cysts, and tumors.

Although breath and qi are commonly viewed as the links between the body and mind, no part is really separate. For example, if you suffer sharp physical pain or you receive a soft, caressing touch, your breathing patterns will change, as will your state of mind. If you have a happy thought or a fearful, panicky one, it will affect both your breathing pattern and your physical body in terms of your tension, posture, and so on. When you are loving and trusting, your shoulders drop and your heart area opens and warms. When you are fearful, your posture is hunched, protective, and tense. We regard all of these responses as automatic and natural, but it is certainly possible to change them with the necessary knowledge, awareness, and practice. Posture and breathing by themselves are unlikely to eradicate ingrained behavioral and thought patterns but they can powerfully assist the process of transformation.

Mind, Sex, and Enlightenment

The last of the Three Regulations is regulation of the mind, or mental dao yin. It is possible to argue that everything we do or refrain from doing is part of regulation of the mind and, in fact, that any discussion of enlightenment is nothing more than the regulation of the mind!

Consider this passage in *The Way to Buddhahood* by the Venerable Yin-shun, regarded by many as one of the leading authorities on modern Chinese Buddhism. The passage is part of an excellent commentary on mindfulness of breathing and in particular on following the breath:

> One follows the breaths up and down and feels them throughout the whole body.... After practicing for a long time, one may feel healthy and strong and have a sensation of warmth in the lower abdomen, or of the breath going all the way to one's heels and toes, or of the breath below the navel going downward to the coccyx and then upward along the spine. Alternatively, when one is breathing in this way, one may have hallucinations of light, forms, sound and so on. All of these experiences are natural physiological phenomena when one's breathing is smooth. Therefore one should not be surprised or boastful: otherwise one will be like those practicing qigong and Taoist alchemy![53]

As both a Buddhist and a qigong practitioner, I would agree wholeheartedly with the above passage except for the last two lines. "Boasting" about energy movement is not a required part of qigong or Daoism, especially since energy movement is taken to be normal. Moreover, in the

above description, from a qigong perspective, the mind is as much leading the qi as it is following the breath. Master Yin-shun is not denying the
existence of qi and seemingly abnormal phenomena, but he seems to be
against knowing how qi works. The balance between doing and not-
doing is always present in Buddhist meditation. Except in practices of
"objectless awareness," the whole samadhi-stream of meditation is based
on concentration wherein an object of meditation is selected and the mind
is focused on it. This is a very active "doing" and may (if one so chooses)
be dismissed as mind manipulation.

If we stand back and take a look at qigong from a broad historic and
spiritual perspective, it should be neither suspicious nor strange. Huston
Smith makes a point of mentioning the Buddha's encounter with raja
yoga during his six years of searching for what would eventually be called
the Middle Way. Smith writes: "His first act was to seek out two of the fore-
most Hindu masters of the day and pick their minds for the wisdom in their
vast tradition. He learned a great deal—about *raja yoga* especially, but
about Hindu philosophy as well; so much in fact that Hindus came to
claim him as their own, holding that his criticisms of the religion of his
day were in the order of reforms and were less important than his agree-
ments.... Having turned his back on mortification, Gautama devoted the
final phase of his quest to a combination of rigorous thought and mystic
concentration along the lines of *raja yoga*."[54]

Smith concludes that the Buddha, "determined to clear the ground
that truth might find new life," stripped away several characteristics
normally associated with religions, namely, authority, ritual, speculation, tradition, divine grace (as opposed to self-effort), and belief in the
supernatural.

The Buddha eventually expressed his spiritual path in eight steps, which,
as we have seen, are often grouped into three "pillars" or "essentials": shila,
samadhi, and pañña, or moral purity, concentration, and wisdom. Raja yoga
training is also broken down into eight steps, which also cover moral purity

and the development of the mind, culminating in samadhi. Buddhists might argue that raja yoga's eight steps do not include wisdom, and raja yoga apologists will probably disagree. According to Vivekananda, "All orthodox systems of Indian philosophy have one goal in view—the liberation of the soul through perfection…. Perfection is always in the Infinite. We are infinite already and we are trying to manifest our infinity."[55] He observed that "He [Buddha] taught the very gist of the philosophy of the Vedas to one and all without distinction; he taught it to the world at large, because one of his great messages was the equality of man." What is beyond argument, however, is that the Buddha's system clearly omits two distinct raja yoga practices—*asana* (postures) and *pranayama* (control of prana).

It would be impossible to say exactly why the Buddha ignored *these,* but it is certainly rash to draw the conclusion that he thought these practices were bad or harmful. After all, according to the Buddha, suffering is caused not by things, people, practices, or ideas *per se,* but by our attachment to them. It is more likely that the Buddha wanted people to focus on the essentials of enlightenment, namely the heart (compassion) and the mind (wisdom). Paravahera Vajiranana Mahathera makes a similar point, from the Theravada Buddhist perspective, in comparing Buddhism and Hinduism:

> Buddhist, unlike the Hindu, systems are directed entirely and exclusively to mental purification and liberation. The Buddha did not teach Bhavana [spiritual development] for the purpose of gaining supernormal powers, the ability to perform prodigious physical feats or to obtain mastery over the external world. He taught with but one object—the extinction of suffering and release from conditioned existence. It is here that we come upon the chief difference between the Buddhist concentration techniques and those commonly associated with Hindu yoga. The latter, particularly Hatha and Raja Yoga, are concerned with results which from the Buddhist standpoint are negligible.[56]

While I would generally agree with the above commentary, two points need to be made. First, very few people, including practicing Buddhists, pursue "liberation" single-mindedly to the exclusion of all else. We occupy ourselves with all sorts of activities that have "negligible" enlightenment results. Second, the restriction of Buddhist spiritual practice to "mental purification" only was long ago modified by the Mahayana and later the Vajrayana streams of Buddhism.

According to a common Mahayana perspective, more emphasis needed to be placed on the heart and the virtue of *karuna*, or compassion. The fate of all people was regarded as interdependent. The bodhisattva postponed personal liberation in order to save all living beings, while lay Buddhists and monks alike began to pray to the bodhisattvas and buddhas for help. Elaborate rituals, replete with concepts of various types of heavens and hells, began to take their place within Buddhist practice. In short, all the elements that the Buddha avoided—authority, ritual, tradition, grace, speculation, and the supernatural—returned.

Within the Chan/Zen tradition, the famous Ten Cow-Herding (or Ox-Herding) Pictures, which depict the various stages of spiritual/consciousness development, are not dissimilar from the Daoist alchemical transformation of jing into qi, qi into shen, shen into the wuji (void), and finally wuji returning into the Dao.

The cow or ox represents your consciousness or true nature. The modern ten pictures are based on brush paintings by a twelfth-century Chan master called Kakuan, who elaborated on an earlier series of six paintings produced during the early Song dynasty (960–1279 C.E.) The descriptions below are loosely based on D.T. Suzuki's, as found in his *Essays in Zen Buddhism*.

1. Looking for the cow. We feel something is missing but we know not what. We have lost sight of our true, inmost nature. We are growing increasingly tired and confused in our search.

2. Discovering the traces of the cow. Through introspection and study of the Dharma, we begin to glimpse an explanation of the mysteries of life and sense that it may indeed be possible that oneness underlies multiplicity.

3. Seeing the cow. Awareness and understanding begin to permeate all activities. We begin to see life in a new light.

4. Catching the cow. We can no longer deny the truth concerning our innate nature, but old habits are strong and we struggle with ourselves.

5. Taming the cow. We must be constantly aware and disciplined in our attempts to control our thoughts and impulses.

6. Riding the cow home. The struggle is finally over. We feel contentment and stop struggling over worldly attainments and matters.

7. The cow is forgotten, leaving the self alone. We have finally arrived "home" and no longer need to think about the cow. All is serene as we sit quietly alone.

8. Both cow and self have disappeared. All is vast emptiness. There is no duality. Even ideas of attainment or holiness are absent.

9. Returning to the source. From the very beginning, we have never really strayed from our source. We can now observe growth and decay, cause and effect, with nonattachment and nonassertion.

10. Returning to everyday life. We can partake the bustle of ordinary life despite our spiritual accomplishments. We need not make a show of our wisdom or power, for they take effect spontaneously.

I think it is significant that picture 8, when both cow and self have disappeared, is depicted by a simple empty circle, which is also used by the Daoists to depict wuji, or the void. The Daoists also talk of "returning to the Source."

In his translation of the *Book of Balance and Harmony*, a classic Daoist anthology from the thirteenth century, Thomas Cleary writes: "[Buddhist] Nirvana and [the Daoist] 'release from the matrix' are but one principle. Release from the matrix means shedding the matrix of mundanity—isn't this nirvana? Taoists refine vitality into energy, refine energy into spirit, refine spirit into emptiness, then embrace the fundamental and return to openness—this is the same principle as the Buddhist teaching of ultimate emptiness."[57] In another Daoist text translated by Cleary, the Daoist understanding of emptiness is elaborated:

> When emptiness is clear, everything thereby flows freely. Therefore ancient sages investigated the beginnings of free flow and stultification, found the source of evolution, forgot form to cultivate energy, forgot energy to cultivate spirit and forgot spirit to cultivate emptiness. Emptiness is truly free-flowing communion. This is called the great sameness. Thus when it is stored it becomes original vitality, when used it becomes myriad consciousness, when relinquished it becomes the absolute one, when let go it becomes the absolute purity.[58]

The main differences between the Buddhists and the Daoists seem to lie not in the ends of their respective practices but in the means. There is still a strong current within Buddhism that elevates the monastic, mind-only approach. Daoism on the other hand embraces the whole being—body, energy, and mind: jing, qi, and shen. The healthy functioning of each part helps the other parts, but in truth the parts are not really separate since they are but artificial concepts. Few people today would question the value of a healthy body, balanced emotions, and a clear, sharp mind. Qigong offers theories and practices, backed in large part by research in traditional Chinese medicine, that provide a "missing link" between mind and body and that fit in with a modern urban lifestyle. It is possible to approach qigong with a raja-yoga-like approach. Try it as a scientific experiment on yourself—with an open mind—and see the reality of qi, what its qualities and dynamics are. Simple exercises can be done safely alone but, as in other forms of internal exploration, it is best to be guided by a qualified teacher. A simple way to feel qi is to hold an imaginary, delicate qi ball in your hands, with the palms facing each other, about 6 to 8 inches apart. Relax you hands and feel a connection between the centers of the palms (called the *laogong* points). Move your hands slowly apart and then back together, keeping a connection between the laogong points, and you will feel the qi ball expanding and contracting. You may be able to feel the qi ball even when your hands are more than a foot apart—too far to claim it is merely body heat. When you are comfortable with your qi ball, you can infuse it with various properties, like heating and cooling it or making its energy spin in different directions. Just use your intent and imagination, or *yi*.

Perhaps the most controversial and misunderstood part of the Daoist alchemical process is the conversion of jing in the form of sexual energy. As we have seen, jing is closely connected with sexual energy and, in men, with the production of sperm. Jing is regarded as the most yin form of qi and naturally flows downward (in the direction of the earth), seeking release in the genitals. One of the most important steps (for men) in the practice of "seminal gongfu" is to refrain from ejaculation and redirect sexual energy up the governing meridian, which runs up the spine, and down the conception meridian, which runs down the front of the body. When these meridians are joined, they constitute the microcosmic orbit referred to above, a major energy circuit in the body. This circulation process is supposed to help nourish and repair the brain and generally slow the aging process. Too much ejaculation depletes the inherited jing and qi, weakening the whole mind-body system. The effects of this depletion are not evident in youth, when there is abundant jing and qi, but become very apparent thereafter, manifesting in loss of vitality, vulnerability to disease, and premature aging, which is so common it is regarded as "normal" aging.

It should be noted that seminal gongfu does not involve the suppression of the sexual urge or of any other emotions, but promotes the transmutation of them into qi. Limiting male ejaculation does not necessarily have to mean limiting the frequency of lovemaking. In sexual gongfu, energy can also be exchanged with a sexual partner with a resulting benefit to both partners.

As we have seen, both tantra and kundalini yoga harness sexual energy in similar ways for transformative purposes, albeit with some differences. They both lead energy up the spine and into the brain but do not circulate it through the microcosmic orbit as in qigong. Traditional raja yoga and kundalini yoga differ from tantra and qigong by recommending that the yogi refrains from sexual activity. All three traditions see their energetic activities as an addition to fundamental spiritual practices—the path of either the heart (bhakti yoga) or head (jnana yoga)—not as a replacement of them.

One translation of opening lines of the Dhammapada reminds us, "All that we are is the result of what we have thought; all that we are is founded on our thoughts and formed of our thoughts."[59] From a qigong perspective this is certainly true, whether we are talking about enlightenment practices, the ability to guide and project qi, emotional and psychological states, or the condition and habits of the physical body. In qigong, it is widely accepted that yi (intention and imagination) leads the qi, which in turn leads the physical body. Thus, as in all systems and traditions, intent is paramount.

Huston Smith sees the maximizing of qi as a common factor in all branches of Daoism:

> The continuum begins with interest in how life's normal allotment
> of *Qi* can be employed to best effect (Philosophical Taoism). From
> there it moves on to ask if that normal quotient can be increased
> (Taoist vitalizing programs). Finally it asks if cosmic energy can
> be gathered, as if by burning glass, to be deployed vicariously for
> the welfare of people who need help (popular or Religious
> Daoism).... A life has substance to the degree that it incorporates
> the profundity of mysticism (Taoist yoga), the direct wisdom of
> gnosis (Philosophical Taoism) and the productive power of magic
> (Religious Taoism).[60]

In the above passage, "Taoist vitalizing programs" and "Taoist yoga"
is the same practice that we have been calling qigong.

Kristofer Schipper, writing from the perspective of an ordained Daoist
priest, points out that, in spite of all the rites and rituals of religious Daoism,
the secret of transformation lies within: "For the Daoist master, the true gods
are found within himself.... The strength that makes one a god lies within
each being. Transcendence is not the result of a spirit separated from matter, an external divine force given to the world, but a spiritualization of *qi*,
of energy-matter itself. Cosmology teaches us that there is nothing that
is not 'matter' and matter cannot be distinguished from its substance, its energy."[61] According to Schipper, religious Daoism regards regulating the qi
as the preliminary stage of the spiritualization process, which is then followed by the stages of "Chaos" and finally "Return." The stage of Chaos
is one of abandonment, letting go of concepts, discipline, and systems. In
the final stage of Return, the union of being and nonbeing, there is no
thought, hearing, or sight, including even ecstatic inner visions.

Medical Qigong Therapy

Before we can complete our overview of qigong, it seems necessary to
shed some light on the confusion that has arisen over the term "medical

qigong therapy." It appears many people use that term to describe the "self-regulation" practices described in the earlier sections of this chapter, on the basis of the fact that they can be used to treat medical problems. While this is absolutely correct, the term "medical qigong therapy" is more precisely used to describe treatment by a specially trained qigong doctor or therapist instead of, or in conjunction with, acupuncture, herbs, or Chinese massage.

A qigong doctor would use the same diagnostic principles and techniques as an acupuncturist or herbalist, but has the additional ability to scan the patient's body and energy fields and to regulate them from a distance. Instead of acupuncture needles, a qigong doctor uses "distance therapy," which is a nontouching/nontactile qi manipulation and emission that "purges" (dissipates or removes), balances, or "tonifies" (builds up) qi in the various parts of the body—organs, meridians, and such. The qigong doctor may also project sound, vibration, and color during such "distance therapy" treatments.

Because a qigong doctor is working with qi, he or she may go directly into organs (which an acupuncturist obviously cannot) and has the ability to bring energy from the external environment to tonify the patient. Accordingly, qigong treatments in a clean, pristine natural environment tend to be more effective.

The distance in "distance therapy" is usually inches or feet away from the patient, but a relatively small number of doctors specialize in treating patients physically situated in other cities or indeed countries.

I do not specialize in such treatments, but I have been requested to perform them a few times and have done so with good results. A particular treatment springs to mind. My patient lived on an island off the West Coast of Canada and was suffering from severe throat cancer, which was very painful and also caused her lungs to fill up with phlegm. I called her by telephone from Toronto to set up the exact time and duration (twenty-five minutes) for the treatment, asking her to lie down comfortably on her bed and relax, as if I were there in person performing the treatment. I imagined she was lying in front of me, and as I scanned her body, I found that the right side of the body was far more affected than the left. I proceeded with the treatment and finished about a minute or two early, since I found my concentration waning. After the treatment, I called her to see what she had experienced. She said that at the appointed starting time of the treatment, her breathing immediately slowed and she started sighing (which, unknown to her, is the sound associated with the lungs and the organs that I first worked on). She felt very relaxed and soothed during the treatment, but a minute or so before the twenty-five minutes had elapsed her breathing suddenly returned to normal. She noticed this because she had set a clock alarm for exactly twenty-five minutes. When I checked up on her a few days later, she said that the pain and the phlegm diminished dramatically for about two days, but then started returning. About two weeks later she left to have surgery in the United States. The utility of working with qi seemed quite clear to me.

In addition to energetic "distance therapy," one of the most important clinical modalities used by qigong doctors is the prescription of self-regulation therapy. This consists of various forms of qigong self-regulation exercises that target a patient's specific condition. Qigong doctors report that the more diligent the patient, the more effective is the treatment.

In my limited experience of observing qigong patients in Chinese hospitals, it seems that they are much more eager to take an active part in returning to good health than their Western counterparts, who have come to expect an effortless, painless, quick-fix pill or other solution. In taking a proactive approach, you accept responsibility for yourself and are no longer a victim of external circumstances. Since mind, energy, and body are all interconnected, this change in attitude in itself is an important part of the cure.

It should be noted that disease, or an imbalance in one's qi, may occur as a result of what Chinese medicine identifies as "external," "internal," or other causes. External causes are due to the climate and include the cold, dampness, dryness, wind, heat, and fire. Internal causes arise from an imbalance in the emotions. Other causes include stress, overexertion, excessive sexual activity, inappropriate diet, parasites, environmental toxins and a weak constitution.

In the case of internal causes, a doctor may correct the resulting qi imbalance, thus making it easier for the patient to work with his or her emotions. Ultimately, however, only the patient can make the requisite changes, despite help from psychologists, psychotherapists, and gurus. It then becomes a matter of mind regulation. The fact that someone has been meditating or carrying on some other spiritual practice for a long time does not safeguard them from emotional imbalance. It depends on the skillfulness, or *gongfu*, of the practitioner.

I regard qigong as extremely useful and helpful knowledge, which I share with those interested. I routinely use qigong in martial arts, to heal myself and to heal others. My overall health and balance undoubtedly aid my "spiritual" practice, although they are in fact inseparable. A common comment by skeptics is, "It's all in the mind!" My reply is: Yes, and isn't that wonderful!

5

Daoist Internal Martial Arts

The Spiritual Warrior

Before we go on to consider the martial applications of qigong, which are interrelated with the Daoist systems of martial arts, it would seem pertinent to explore the broader connections between spirituality and fighting, whether we think of the subject in a sense that is individual or collective, figurative or physical.

The concept of the spiritual warrior seems to have caught the popular imagination and is used in a surprising variety of situations—from abstaining from that extra cup of cappuccino to attempting to bring down the very structure of modern Western civilization. In the interests of simplicity, we may say the term "spiritual warrior" is used in two main contexts, namely, to describe one's internal spiritual struggle and to describe an external struggle—whether political, military, or religious.

Both contexts are determined by our interpretation of self, god, and spirituality; and in the modern world these are dominated by the interrelated Western religions of Judaism, Christianity, and Islam. The impact of Western religious ideas and attitudes is reinforced not only by the dominance of Western, especially American, popular culture but also by sheer numbers. Followers of Christianity and Islam account for more than half of the world's current population of six billion.

Western religious concepts are so widespread that many people regard them as universal although they are in fact quite particular. In terms of global mythology and religion, the Genesis story of a sudden Creation, Fall, and eventual Redemption, as well as the cosmic battle between Good and Evil, was a departure from the ancient idea of endless cycles of creation, destruction, and renewal. God was no longer seen as immanent in all creation but was a separate, almighty (but humanlike) being, who made humans from the earth and constantly tested their goodness or sinfulness. In addition, this new god was not a universal deity, caring equally for all creation, but was very much tribal, concerned with protecting and furthering his particular tribe. As Karen Armstrong writes, "Yahweh did not remain the cruel and violent god of the Exodus, even though the myth has been important in all three of the monotheistic religions. Surprising as it may seem, the Israelites would transform him beyond recognition into a symbol of transcendence and compassion. Yet the bloody story of the Exodus would continue to inspire dangerous conceptions of the divine and a vengeful theology.... The myth of a Chosen People and a divine election has often inspired a narrow, tribal ideology from the time of the Deuteronomist right up to the Jewish, Christian and Muslim fundamentalism that is unhappily rife in our own day."[62]

In the forms of popular religion as described above, belief is a major factor. God's wishes are conveyed to his people through his chosen prophets, whether Abraham, Moses, Jesus, or Muhammad, and written down and interpreted by subsequent followers, often centuries later. A spiritual warrior of such a tradition would try to follow God's wishes and instructions in his or her own inner life and, externally, would jealously guard orthodoxy and continuity of belief, which is cast in uncompromising terms of good and evil, saved and damned. In psychological terms, when one identifies with a belief a threat to that belief is a threat to the believer, and this lends itself to extremism since believers feel personally threatened by other belief systems. In the cases of Christianity and Islam, the defense of belief has for more than a thousand years led to the imposition of belief, often by brutal force of arms. Christians have conducted crusades against the Muslims, persecuted the Jews throughout Europe, and sent missionaries all over the world to "save souls," usually accompanied by colonization and the harvesting of riches. Even today in America, few people question the practice of sending troops into battle around the world while invoking God's blessing and support, seemingly regardless of the political decisions behind deployment. We still hear our leaders describe conflict in simplistic terms: "with us or against us," "battle between good and evil," and the like.

In contrast to this popular Western religion, the wisdom traditions regard the divine as both transcendent and immanent (present in all creation, human or otherwise). There is a recurring cycle of involution and evolution, whereby spirit, God, or Dao loses itself in gross matter and slowly rediscovers itself through the processes of evolution and enlightenment. The Ten Cow-Herding Pictures and the transformation of jing into qi into shen are descriptions of the evolutionary process. The descent of wuji into taiji (yin and yang) is the description of the involutionary process.

Since these traditions teach self-transformation and the evolution of consciousness rather than conformity to belief, it would make no sense to try to spread enlightenment by the sword, whip, or gun. History seems to support the logic of this. The oldest wisdom traditions, Hinduism, Buddhism, and Daoism, have inspired comparatively little military conquest despite being practiced by large, relatively advanced civilizations. Hinduism has stayed in India, and Daoism in China, while Buddhism has spread mostly eastward from India, not by armies but gradually through the efforts of individual teachers.

It is important to point out that wisdom traditions exist within the Western religions, mostly as so-called mystic sects, like the Gnostics and Cathars in Christianity, the Sufis in Islam, and the Kabbalists in Judaism. The major flowering of Western mysticism took place between the eleventh and fourteenth centuries. In terms of the Hindu classification of the four major yogas, or paths to God—bhakti, jnana, karma, and raja—Western mysticism is regarded by many Hindu scholars as forms of bhakti yoga. In the early stages of bhakti, we see God as separate and superior, but in the later stages we realize that we and God are one in nature and that we can realize divinity within ourselves by transforming our consciousness. We use emotions, especially love, to propel ourselves into and along this transformational process.

A spiritual warrior in the ageless wisdom tradition wages an inner battle with hatred and illusion and aspires to enlightenment and unity with the divine, the Absolute. The struggle is not totally internal, however, because, even though spirit is transcendent, it is also immanent. Even though the world is just a passing play or illusion, it nevertheless has meaning, and the spiritual warrior is called to make decisions and act in the everyday world. The Christian mystic Pope Gregory the Great (540–604), describing his own internal battle to move to a more enlightened consciousness, writes that the soul "cannot fix its mind's eye on that which it has with hasty glance seen within itself, because it is compelled by its own habits to sink downwards. It meanwhile pants and struggles and endeavors to go above itself but sinks back, overpowered with weariness, into its own familiar darkness."[63]

The term *jihad*, which is currently used by many Muslims to mean "holy war," in the sense of an armed conflict or even an act of terrorism, originally referred to an internal spiritual struggle. Armstrong writes:

> The mystic was engaged in a ceaseless struggle *(jihad)* to distinguish the compassion, love and beauty of God in all things and to

strip away everything else. The *Masnawi* [Sufi "bible"] challenged the Muslim to find the transcendent dimension in human life and to see through appearances to the hidden reality within. It is the ego which blinds us to the inner mystery of all things, but once we have got beyond that we are not isolated, separate beings but one with the Ground of all existence.[64]

Perhaps the most famous discussion of spirituality and warfare is to be found in the Bhagavad Gita, written around the sixth century C.E. The Gita begins as Arjuna, the leader of the Pandavas, has doubts about going into battle against his war-mongering cousins, the Kauravas, and is looking to the Lord Krishna for advice. In the quotes below, taken from Annie Besant's classic translation, Arjuna despondently complains: "Teachers, fathers, sons as well as grandfathers, mother's brothers, fathers-in-law, grandsons, brothers-in-law and other relatives. These I do not wish to kill though myself slain, even for the sake of the kingship of the three worlds, how then for earth?... Alas in committing a great sin are we engaged, we who are endeavoring to kill our kindred from greed of the pleasures of kingship."[65]

Krishna begins his discourse by acknowledging Arjuna's wisdom and compassion but pointing out the difference between the body and the soul: "Thou grievest for those that should not be grieved for, yet speakest words of wisdom. The wise grieve neither for the living nor the dead.... As the dweller in the body experienceth in the body childhood, youth, old age, so passeth he on to another body; the steadfast one grieveth not thereat."

Vivekananda, who described the Gita as a "bouquet composed of the beautiful flowers of spiritual truths collected from the Upanishads," feels the *Gita*'s most valuable lessons concern work and activity (karma):

> The doctrine which stands out luminously on every page of the
> Gita is that of intense activity, but in the midst of it, eternal

> calmness.... All work is by nature composed of good and evil....
> Good action will produce good effects; bad action, bad. But good
> and bad are both bondages of the soul. The solution reached in the
> Gita in regard to the bondage-producing nature of work is that,
> if we do not attach ourselves to the work we do, it will not have
> any binding effect on our soul. This is the one central idea in the
> Gita: work incessantly, but be not attached.[66]

In characterizing the fighting Shaolin monks according to the above terms, they would be spiritual warriors belonging to the path of Ageless Wisdom spirituality. We would expect them to be full of compassion, one of Buddhism's twin virtues. They would perform "right action" with an inner calm and emptiness, in a manner similar to that described in the Bhagavad Gita or to the Daoists' non-action.

From what we know of legend and history, the Shaolin monks did indeed act in the above manner, garnering a widespread and lasting reputation for justice, wisdom, and caring. They did not participate in conquest, whether for religious or political reasons, but fought only in self-defense to protect their temples, the local populace, and their country when invaded or beset by foreign marauders. Shaolin codes of conduct stipulated that "boxing" be used only for self-defense and not for greed, bullying, or boastful display. The monks were of course subject to the usual monks' precepts such as the abstention from sex, meat, and wine.

Internal and External Martial Arts
Although the Shaolin martial arts tradition became extremely influential in China and throughout the Far East, it was not the only such tradition. As we saw in the previous chapter, over two thousand years ago, well before the founding of the Shaolin Temple, the martial arts in China became associated with the development of qi and with the cultivation of virtue.

It has become common to contrast the Shaolin system and its many offshoots with the Daoist-inspired martial arts systems, which are variously described as "soft," "internal," or "Wudang," after the famous Daoist temple on Wudang Mountain in Hubei Province. Three main forms of martial arts are recognized as "internal": taijiquan *(tai chi chuan)*, baguazhang *(pa kua chang)*, and xingyiquan *(hsing i chuan)*. The romanization used in the parentheses above, which may be more familiar to readers, is the Wade-Giles system. Throughout this book, I have attempted to use the more modern Pinyin system, which was developed in China in 1958 and is becoming the increasingly universal standard.

The theoretical foundations of all three internal martial arts are based on the principles of the yin-yang and Five Elements theories as reformulated by the Dao Xue, or Neo-Confucianists, who consciously started combining the philosophies of Confucianism, Daoism, and Buddhism around the ninth century. The Wudang systems openly acknowledge the contributions of the Shaolin Temple to their arts in terms of martial techniques but tend to be more reticent as regards the philosophy, which they insist is pure Daoism.

Taijiquan is based on the yin-yang theory as described by Zhou Dunyi's famous *taiji tu* (yin-yang diagram), which was produced during the eleventh century. This in itself is remarkable since most martial systems are based on practical techniques rather than philosophical theories. *Taiji* in "taijiquan" thus refers to the interaction of yin and yang, but it literally means "supreme ultimate"; and *quan* is translated as "fist" or "boxing." As we have seen, yin-yang theory is a unique cornerstone of Chinese culture and philosophy.

Baguazhang, which means "Eight Trigrams palm," is based, as the name may suggest, on the theory of the Eight Trigrams. A trigram consists of three lines stacked one above the other. These lines are either solid, representing the yang element, or broken, representing the yin. They depict the eight major interactions of yin and yang, in much the same way that the six-line hexagrams depict the sixty-four more detailed interactions of yin and yang. Both the trigrams and hexagrams are to be found in the ancient classic of legendary times, the *Yi Jing (I Ching)*.

Xingyiquan literally means "form-mind fist." *Xing* refers to external shape or form, while *yi*, which we have already encountered in our discussion of qigong, means mind or intention. This implies that the intention comes first and is directly and accurately manifested in physical action. Xingyiquan is based on five "fists," or ways of striking, which represent the five elements or phases of the Five Elements, or Five Phases, theory. The generating (or creating) and controlling cycles of the Five Elements theory is used to determine the responsive combat strategies of xingyiquan in much the same way as it is used in traditional Chinese medicine to respond to pathogens.

Robert Smith and Donn Draeger, in their *Asian Fighting Arts*, comment on an obscure manuscript attributed to Zhang Sanfeng, the legendary founder of taijiquan, in which he lists the differences between the internal systems *(nei jia)* and the external *(wai jia):* "External—stressed the regulation of breath, training of bones and muscles, ability to advance and retreat and unity of hard and soft. Internal—emphasized the training of bones and muscles, exercise of qigong, subduing the offensive by stillness and had the aim of defeating an enemy the instant he attacked. Even though this distinction cannot be confirmed, it tends to erase some misconceptions on the differences between the systems. Both systems had what are usually considered external as well as internal characteristics."[67]

Some claim that "internal" actually refers to training inside the temple as opposed to the world outside and would thus imply esotericism. Others claim it refers to *neigong* (internal skill), which would be, more or less, qigong. The Shaolin systems have their own forms of qigong, but it is difficult to determine when these started. It is not unlikely that some of these were borrowed from the Daoists.

The modern "internal" martial arts all blossomed together during the nineteenth century. Modern taijiquan traces its roots directly back to a martial art taught within the Chen family in their village in Henan Province, not too far from the original Song Shan Shaolin Temple. The first person outside the Chen family to learn this art was Yang Luochan (1799–1872), who was taught by Master Chen Changxin. In time, Yang simplified its movements and performed them in a softer, rounder manner, emphasizing its many health maintenance aspects. He went to Beijing to teach around 1862, and here his popularity soon caught the attention of the royal family. When some members of the royal family started to learn taijiquan from Yang, its popularity spread across China and subsequently around the world.

About the same time that Yang Luochan was learning the Chen family style, Li Luoneng (1808–90, also called Li Nengran) was learning a style called *xinyiquan* (heart-mind fist) from Master Dai Wenxun. After ten years of study, Li created a modified style of martial arts, which he called xingyiquan (form-mind fist), which was similar in sound but different in meaning. Li began teaching this new style around 1856. He produced excellent students, including Liu Qilan and the famous Guo Yunshen, whose nickname was Divine Crushing Hand.

Toward the end of the nineteenth century, certain prominent teachers of xingyiquan, baguazhang, and taijiquan agreed to share their arts with each others' students since there was so much common ground among the three styles. They called these three arts *nei jia,* or "internal family," of Chinese martial arts.

Most sources point to Dong Haichuan (1813–83) as the creator or first famous teacher of baguazhang. In 1865, shortly after Yang Luochan started teaching in Beijing, Dong was invited to teach his art in the household of Prince Su. Dong had many brilliant students who became famous in their own right.

A widely circulated story relates that Divine Crushing Hand Guo, on learning of Dong's spreading fame in Beijing, challenged him to a bare-hands duel. Dong would not have taken this challenge lightly, since Guo had been a professional bounty hunter and had spent three years in jail for killing an armed bandit with his bare hands. The story tells that Guo attacked for two whole days, using xingyiquan, which is a very powerful and direct style. Dong neutralized this using the nimble, circular stepping and coiling techniques for which baguazhang is famous. On the third day of the duel (they rested at night), Dong went on the offensive and defeated Guo. After that duel, they became lifelong friends and agreed that they would request their students to learn both baguazhang and xingyiquan, since they were both excellent arts, and were based on similar principles.

The legendary three-day duel may or may not have actually occurred, but there were probably meetings, social gatherings, discussions, and closed-door "testing of skills." Whatever actually transpired, it is a historical fact that high-level xingyiquan masters began learning baguazhang, and vice versa. Among the first to start this crossover trend were the xingyiquan masters Li Cunyi and Geng Jishan (Li's cousin), who were disciples of Liu Qilan. Geng was the wushu "grandfather" of my own teacher, Miss Rose Li (he taught her teacher, Deng Yunfeng). Although Li Cunyi is listed in the official baguazhang records as a disciple of Dong, he probably learned from Dong's senior disciple, Cheng Tinghua. It is said that Cheng studied some xingyiquan from Guo Yunshen after he had studied baguazhang with Dong. Cheng, Guo, and Li Cunyi were all friends and natives of Shen County, Hebei Province.

One of the most famous "internal family" martial artists of modern times is Sun Lutang, who created one of the five modern taijiquan styles, the Sun style. Dan Miller writes in a recent translation of Sun Lutang's book *Xingyiquan Xue* about the coming together of taijiquan, baguazhang, and xingyiquan:

The first known grouping of these arts under the name "internal family" occurred in 1894. Baguazhang master Cheng Tinghua and his friends, Liu Dekuan, Li Cunyi and Liu Weixiang, came together to form an organization of martial artists in order to improve the level of their arts, increase harmony within the martial arts circles and raise the skill level of their students.... The group originally called it *Nei Jia Quan* (Internal Family Boxing). Later, after it was discovered there had previously been an art called *Nei Jia Quan,* the name was changed to *Nei Gong Quan* (Internal Skill Boxing), however it was too late and the name Nei Jia Quan had stuck.[68]

Taijiquan

The most widely recognized of the internal martial arts is undoubtedly taijiquan, commonly known in the West as "tai chi." It is seen in every public park in China and increasingly in parks throughout the world. It is a mass-participation activity that will probably soon become an Olympic sport and is steadily making its way into community centers and seniors' homes. Some Western doctors are beginning to prescribe it as a form of therapy as Western medical evidence accumulates. Research is a slow process since there is at present not much profit in preventative health care. In a recently published study, doctors at Tufts-New England Medical Center analyzed forty-seven studies on taijiquan and found that it could indeed help with balance, flexibility, heart health, arthritis, pain, anxiety, and stress.

In spite of its steadily growing popularity, however, taijiquan remains little understood. The modern lifestyle leaves us perpetually short of time, so we generally do not want something that seems too complex. We want just the results, please—which in the case of taijiquan are its reputed health maintenance and vitality. As a consequence of this market pressure, taijiquan "forms" (sequences of movements) have grown shorter, and many of those teaching taijiquan undergo less and less personal training—sometimes just a weekend. Indeed, I have even received a solicitation to learn a five-minute tai chi routine, which I was promised would make me a lot of money. This is a pity because the secret of taijiquan's mysterious benefits lies as much in the intention *(yi)* behind the physical movements as in the shape *(xing)* of those movements. The adage in qigong that the yi, or intention, guides the qi, which in turn guides the physical body, applies no less to taijiquan and the other internal martial arts—not to mention meditation and the rest of our lives. In our scramble for the "quick fix," we may be casting aside one of humanity's true pearls. Lasting skill, or gongfu, in any endeavor requires persistence, intelligence, and time.

The legendary founder of taijiquan was Zhang Sanfeng, who supposedly was born during the late Song dynasty (960–1279). He is said to have mastered Shaolin Quan early in life and, after a career in government service, wandered through China's mountains looking for sages to teach him. He did eventually meet a Daoist master and spent nine years in the Wudang Mountains, practicing what he had learned. It is said that the famous Daoist temple on Wudang Mountain was built in his honor. Its construction started in 1412.

Some sources claim that Zhang was inspired to create taijiquan as a result of a dream, while others insist that it was after he had witnessed a bird and a snake fighting. He was struck by the effectiveness of the subtle but powerful and always circular movements of the snake's body.

The most likely explanation was that the legendary Zhang (or other actual innovators) found that the basic techniques of Shaolin Quan could be improved or at least made more effective with less brute strength through the application of yin-yang principles and qigong, which, as we have seen, includes the regulations of posture, breathing, and mind. This would have been a logical extension of the philosophical intermingling between Buddhism and Daoism that had been taking place during the preceding centuries.

Having myself studied Shaolin Quan, I could not see, during the first few years of my taijiquan practice, how taijiquan could be more effective than Shaolin Quan in a real combat or self-defense situation. When I came to Canada and no longer had the benefit of Miss Li's instructions, I looked to the *Dao De Jing* and the taiji classics for guidance. Eventually, through Master Jerry Alan Johnson, I began to understand qigong, which was the missing piece of an amazingly powerful and effective puzzle. Looking back at those times, I was glad that I was forced, through the absence of a physical teacher, to study the taiji classics because I have come to realize that those writings, far from being merely fanciful, poetic, or symbolic, describe an actual state of being. You do not merely apply taiji principles, you embody them, becoming a living, breathing three-dimensional yin-yang symbol. It reminds me of something Miss Li once said to me: "In the beginning, you do taijiquan, but if you practice, eventually taijiquan does you." The same can be said of the breath in meditation.

Although various lineages, including some within the Wudang system, claim direct links with Zhang Sanfeng, historians have not been able to verify them. In this absence, most people today regard the Chen family as the originators of modern taijiquan, and in particular Chen Wangting, who started teaching this new system around the beginning of the Qing dynasty in 1644. In addition to various sets of "shadow boxing," or solo patterns of movements, Chen Wangting also taught "push hands" *(tui shou)* techniques, which are practiced with a partner in order to develop various combat skills including sensing, sticking, following, continuity, and issuing power. Tui shou is at first usually performed as a stationary, cooperative drill and later can progress to moving, fast striking, and *chinna*, which includes joint locking and takedowns.

Chen-style taijiquan has been streamlined over the centuries but is still widely practiced today, although it is not as popular as the slower and less martial-seeming Yang style. Chen-style taijiquan gave rise not only to Yang style but also to the Wu-family style, which features smaller, more compact movements. Yang style in turn gave rise to the Wu style, named after Wu Jianquan. Sun Lutang created the Sun style, which incorporated elements of xingyiquan and baguazhang. The writings of the great teachers from all these styles, together with some writings attributed to Zhang Sanfeng, make up what are called the Taiji Classics. Even though there are many stylistic variations within taijiquan, all forms of taijiquan should conform to the principles laid out in the Taiji Classics. Serious taijiquan students are strongly advised to consider what they are being taught in the light of the Taiji Classics.

Taijiquan is unique and remarkable because it is an extremely effective martial art, a moving meditation, a mind-body exercise, and a physical expression of Daoist yin-yang philosophy, all wrapped in a beautiful package of dancelike movement. It would seem to be a marketer's dream in our time-conscious and health-conscious modern world. The marketing drawback is that there are no dramatic short-term results, no guarantee of zero-fat abs and buns of steel or the ability to magically fly through the air. Cultivation of gongfu requires an investment of time (even if just half an hour a day) before taijiquan and life itself begin to seem effortless.

Taijiquan can be very crudely characterized as a fusion of external martial arts (wushu, karate, etc.), meditation, and yoga. As a form of qigong, it covers much of the same ground as hatha yoga and pranayama yoga. Taijiquan auxiliary exercises include yoga-like stretching and breathing, which are utilized during the performance of the taijiquan "form" but these are internalized and thus not apparent to most observers. Advanced taijiquan practitioners can also direct qi within and around the body as they practice their form. Thus the slow, innocuous-looking (and in the

West, often mocked) taijiquan player in the park may actually be nourishing particular organs, drawing energy from the environment, or developing power that can break bones with only an inch of movement.

Taijiquan is different from yoga because of its martial applications and the fact that it is much more dynamic, with the whole body moving continuously without ever stopping. Circularity is vital to maintaining fluidity, since without it movements will be a series of stops and starts, no matter how subtly disguised. *The Theory of Taijiquan,* attributed to Zhang Sanfeng, states:

> In any action, the whole body should be light and agile, or *Ching* and *Lin*. One should feel that all of the body's joints are connected with full linkage. *Chi* should be stirred. The spirit of vitality, or *Shen*, should be concentrated inwards. Do not show any deficiency, neither concavity nor convexity in movement. Do not show disconnected movement. The *Chin* [a type of qi] is rooted in the feet, bursts out in the legs, is controlled by the waist and functions through the fingers. From the feet to the legs, legs to the waist, all should be moved as one unit.... Long quan, like a great river, flows unceasingly.[69]

If you succeed in carrying out the above instructions, then your body and movements will begin to resemble a dynamic, three-dimensional yin-yang diagram, rolling on and intermingling and balancing yin and yang continuously. For example, if you take a video of yourself and review it in slow motion, then no part of your body should ever stop once you commence your taijiquan form—hands, arms, torso, or legs. Your knees and elbows must remain bent or else they will straighten and lock, causing your movements to become jerky and unbalanced. This is not as easy to accomplish as it may first seem.

In 1998, in order to draw attention to the widespread incidence of falling among seniors and our general need to defuse stress by slowing down, I proposed a new world record attempt to the *Guinness Book of World Records,* and they accepted it. It would be a "race" to see who would be the slowest person to cover ten meters, with at least one part of the lower body always in forward movement. Two races, open to the public, were run in 1998 and 1999, attracting competitors with varied backgrounds including athletics, martial arts, ballet, and yoga. The eventual winner was one of my students and an instructor, Ken Poole. Ken, who was sixty-one at the time, beat back much younger competitors with an astounding time of 54 minutes and 30 seconds, or about one foot of forward movement every two minutes. The reader may try this for fun, but be warned: no tottering is allowed since this involves backward movement!

Training yourself according to yin-yang principles causes you to take on the characteristics of an energetic ball or a series of linked wheels. Each of the three internal arts is likened to a different kind of energetic ball. Taijiquan, being the most yin and defensive of the three, has been likened to a bouncing ball, which can be observed in the taijiquan form through the repeated shifting of the weight backward and forward. If you push against a big ball, it will either spin you off to the side or else rebound directly into you. The harder you strike it, the faster it will roll or rebound. The ball will respond this way not as an act of self-defense or retaliation but because that is its nature. So it is with the taijiquan master.

As an example of this sort of dynamic is one of the tactics used in taijiquan *tui shou* practice, called by some "the swinging door." Since in taijiquan the torso is kept relaxed and loose with the spine straight, when someone pushes against your left side, it will yield naturally like a swinging door. This will not only dissipate incoming force, but the turning may cause the attacking weapon (e.g., fingers and hand) to be caught and twisted by the circular motion, somewhat like putting your hand into a fan or turning wheel. In addition, the harder and faster the left side is pushed the harder and faster the right side swings forward. This forward movement may be converted into a strike, arm break, or takedown without much conscious intention since the body is merely conducting the attacker's own force. The quantity, speed, and direction of the returning force will depend on the exact nature of the attacking force.

It would actually be an oversimplification to describe taijiquan energetics as a ball or even as a set of geared wheels since energy is directed by the mind and is not limited by fixed physical dimensions of either the energy "ball" or of the taijiquan player's body. Since humans are linked with both heaven and earth, we can move energy in and out of the ground as well as space. An advanced taijiquan player can create many interlinked circles of energy within the body, and these are capable of being suddenly propelled outward, outside the body. Conversely, force coming into the body can be deflected into these circuits, somewhat like a shock absorber. The writings of the Chen-style school discusses the cultivation of *chansijin*, which has been translated as "pulling the silk" or as "spiral-coiling" energy. Master Jou Tsunghwa writes: "Chan-ssu Chin *[Chansijin]* seeks to unify the curved and the straight, which are opposites. Like a bullet which revolves on its own axis and simultaneously follows a parabolic trajectory…the Chan-ssu Chin operates by forming a spiral line in space…. Tai-Chi appears to be propelled by a big moving screw inside the body. Cheng Man-Ching, perhaps the greatest Tai-Chi Chuan master known by Westerners, always reminded his students to make their hands and head move as part of the body and not independently."[70]

There are many other principles of taijiquan practice, but I will just briefly mention a few more since my purpose is not to instruct but to give the readers a sense of what taijiquan is (or is not—for example, a martial ballet or slow-moving karate). Taijiquan incorporates and harmonizes many pairs of seeming opposites—wuji and taiji, heaven (rising, light) and earth (sinking, rooted), doing and non-doing, substantial and insubstantial, inside and outside, front and back.

An important quality in taijiquan is sensitivity and awareness. Wu Yuxiang, the creator of Wu-family style, advised: "In standing, the body should be erect and relaxed, able to respond immediately to an attack from any direction. One's appearance should be like a hawk swooping down upon its prey; the spirit should be like a cat mousing. It rests like a mountain; it flows like the current of a river.... If your opponent does not move, you should remain still. But at his slightest move, you should be ahead of him."[71]

Sensitivity grows out of stillness. If the mind is distracted, fearful, and jumpy, it will be slow to sense external movement. If the body is tense or committed in a certain direction or attitude (e.g., attacking or retreating), it cannot respond spontaneously because it is already programmed. In taijiquan, "sensitivity" includes reading the very intention to attack through extremely subtle physical and energetic movements within the opponent. This sensitivity can work even blindfolded and at a distance.

One of the things about taijiquan *tui shou* (push hands) practice that still amazes me is how precisely it can demonstrate complex philosophical yin-yang principles in a physical manner. All of the above discussions about energy balls, sensitivity, pulling and pushing, attacking and defending, continuity, circularity, and so on can be applied to any aspect of our lives, since life is relationship and yin-yang theory is about the dynamics of relationship.

In modern America, for example, it has become fashionable at many different levels, individual as well as collective, to flaunt power and an aggressive win-at-all-costs attitude. If more people experienced even a little "push hands" practice, they would be much more humble and cautious because they would realize how quickly and completely the tables can be turned on blind, brute force.

In addition to the taijiquan solo form, push hands, and various qigong practices, an advanced practitioner would also be expected to understand taiji philosophy. It is also usual to practice a weapons form, of which the most common and beautiful is the taiji double-edged straight sword *(jian)*. Some medical qigong therapists prescribe the repetition of specific taijiquan movements as part of their treatment, since they are related to particular energetics or organs within the body.

Baguazhang

In terms of the three main internal martial arts, baguazhang is often viewed as the middle one, halfway between the defensive and yielding taijiquan and the directly advancing xingyiquan. Some describe the internal martial arts as different parts of a dragon, with taijiquan being the tail, baguazhang the waist, and xingyiquan the head. Baguazhang is likened to a spinning energy ball or to a tornado because of its constant circling foot movements and its coiling and twisting body movements, which resemble a circling dragon.

Baguazhang is unique in its appearance, since one of its main training practices and combat strategies is circle walking around an opponent. Baguazhang fighters are in continual movement and can change direction, attack, or defend without stopping to plant the feet, thereby presenting an elusive, unpredictable target. Because a skilled baguazhang fighter tends to circle to avoid an attack, aggressive fighters, especially if bigger, sometimes make the mistake of presuming he or she is a coward or cannot attack. This is a major error because in baguazhang, as in the other internal martial arts, fighters strike with the force of the whole body, not just by swinging the arms or legs. Because of all the internal energetic circling (similar to taijiquan's *chansijin*), baguazhang is able to deliver surprising power from extremely short distances and unexpected angles, and with surprising speed. No "windup" is necessary.

Muhammad Ali, perhaps the greatest heavyweight boxer of all time, famously described his strategy in terms that a baguazhang fighter would applaud: "Float like a butterfly and sting like a bee." What set him apart from other boxers was his unusual hand and foot speed, his mobility, and his ability to slip away from punches with slight shifts of his relaxed body. When his speed and stamina began to fail, he compensated with intelligence and spirit *(shen)*. I, for one, would vote him an honorary baguazhang hero.

It is not surprising that movement and change are the strengths of baguazhang because its theoretical basis is the Bagua, or Eight Trigrams, that describe the eight main variations of yin-yang interaction. As has been explained previously, a *gua* is a diagram made up on three lines, one above the other, which are either broken (yin) or solid (yang). In their book *Baguazhang*, masters Liang, Yang, and Wu write:

> The Bagua is a theory (expressed in a diagram) which was used
> by the ancient Chinese to analyze directions, locations, causes
> and effects and all natural changes of the universe. Since nature
> always repeats itself, the Chinese believe that Bagua theory can
> be used to predict natural disasters, a country's destiny or even
> an individual's fortune.... As martial artists, if we understand and
> follow the natural patterns of *qi* circulating in our bodies and
> around us in nature, we will be able to manifest our own *qi* and
> strength more efficiently and powerfully.[72]

There are two arrangements of the trigrams as used in the Bagua—Pre-Heaven, or Early Heaven, and Post-Heaven, or Later Heaven. The Pre-Heaven Bagua symbol is attributed to Fu Xi of the Legendary Period, who is thought to have lived between 2950 and 2840 B.C.E. The Post-Heaven Bagua is attributed to Wen Wang, the first ruler of Zhou dynasty (1122–256 B.C.E.), who is also credited with creating the *Yi Jing*, which is sometimes called in China the *Zhou Yi* or the *Zhou Book of Changes*. When they are shown together, the Pre-Heaven Bagua is on the inside. If the outside Post-Heaven Bagua is rotated one trigram at a time, the sixty-four hexagrams of the *Yi Jing* are produced.

The Pre-Heaven Bagua depicts primordial balance and order, with the symbolic opposites placed directly across from each other. Thus, the most yang trigram, three solid lines, representing Heaven, would be placed at the top of the diagram, while the most yin, three divided lines, representing Earth, would be placed at the bottom, directly across from Heaven. The Post-Heaven Bagua depicts the major dynamics within the human world of time and space. The names given to the eight basic trigrams are Heaven, Earth, Thunder, Water, Mountain, Wind, Fire, and Lake.

In baguazhang, the Bagua is used to analyze the relationships between different parts of the body and between different types of fighters, based on their temperament and physical constitution. In the system created by Sun Lutang, for example, the most yang fighter is represented by the lion, which is extremely strong and aggressive. The most yin is the mythical unicorn, which is gentle by nature and capable of flight. Unicorn fighters are adept at spinning around on one leg. The other animals within this system are the snake, falcon, dragon, bear, phoenix, and monkey. The snake is soft on the outside but strong inside, capable of hitting vital points with speed. The falcon can spin with great speed. The dragon is associated with thunder, externally still but active on the inside, capable of sudden explosion and unpredictable change. The bear is docile by nature but very strong and extremely dangerous when roused. The phoenix swirls like a tornado, keeping the upper body firm but the lower parts flexible. The monkey is very agile, with the ability to crouch low and then suddenly leap. I have found this system useful, since some fighters exhibit both the physique and personalities of these animals, even the mythical ones.

Apart from the circle walking, the most distinctive feature of baguazhang is its "overturning palm," *(fan zhang)*, which also forms the basis of other, more complex "changes." In contrast to taijiquan and xingyiquan, baguazhang uses the open palm *(zhang)* rather than the closed fist *(quan)*. In the standard "guard" stance, the lead hand is held with the palm facing outward, fingertips at eyebrow level, protecting the head and upper body. The space between the thumb and first finger is open and is called the "tiger's mouth," serving as a sort of gun sight as the baguazhang fighter circles. The rear hand is also held palm outward, its fingertips a few inches below the elbow of the lead arm, protecting the midsection of the body—solar plexus, stomach, and ribs.

As the baguazhang player faces an opponent, both hands cover the centerline of the body, preventing a straight strike down the middle. This is extremely important, because it forces an attacker to take the longer route around the centerline. The fact that both elbows are bent and pointing toward the ground (as in taijiquan) even during a forward strike, makes it difficult for an opponent to attack the midsection. The common "corkscrew" punch, seen in Shaolin Quan, karate, and taekwondo, is more or less at right angles to the torso, leaving a much wider-open area for counterattack.

The "overturning palm" *(fan zhang)* is a way of changing palms (with the back hand replacing the front hand and vice versa) without leaving any opening for counterattack. As the front hand withdraws, it pulls back and down toward the center; the rear hand spirals up and down as it strikes forward. When done continuously, they resemble a spinning ball. During the fan zhang the hands perform the four basic movements of baguazhang: rise *(qi)*, drill *(zuan)*, fall *(luo)*, and overturn *(fan)*. These are similar to (but not exactly the same as) the four basic movements of taijiquan: ward off *(peng)*, pull back *(lu)*, press *(ji)*, and push *(an)*. Even though the above descriptions relate mainly to the arms and hands, it must be remembered that in the internal arts the whole body is interconnected and linked. Thus even when the fan zhang is performed with the feet stationary, the energy ripples from the feet through the torso to the arms and hands—like a dragon riding the winds or waves.

It is common to walk the Bagua circle with the arms held in a guard stance (as described above), with the torso turned toward the center of the circle, as if circling an imaginary opponent. In this position, no vulnerable target areas are exposed. Most forms of baguazhang include various "changes" (usually eight in number), that enable the baguazhang player to change direction while dealing with various kinds of imaginary attacks.

There are three heights, or "basins" *(pen)*, of walking in baguazhang. The high basin is normal walking height and is used for speed, especially if the body is out of reach of the opponent's weapons. During the middle-basin walking, the body is slightly squatting, and the "root" (stability by sinking into the ground) is stronger, enabling strong contact with the opponent. The lower-basin walking is used to train leg strength and qigong. Traditional teachers made their students walk and perform "lower basin" maneuvers under tables.

Baguazhang is surprisingly fast, even for seasoned martial artists, because of the speed and turning ability of the footwork and because the strike is issued as part of the stepping. The Bagua fighter can wait until the last moment before committing—even after making energetic or (extremely light) physical contact with the opponent, allowing the fighter to sense the exact direction and power of the attack. In most styles of martial arts, the fighter drops into a stance and then launches a punch or kick. Even if this is done very fast, it means that the attack must be decided beforehand and that energy must be used to "apply brakes," create a stable foundation, and then generate some sort of swing, usually from the hips, to launch a kick or punch.

If we use a baseball analogy to compare other styles of martial arts with the internal arts including baguazhang, we would say the former is like a batter who guesses the location of a ball and commits to a mighty swing in that area. In the Bagua approach, on the contrary, he is like a batter who can stay back long enough to see precisely how the ball is approaching before hitting it, resulting in a far higher and more consistent batting average. In military terms, an attack in other styles is like a ballistic missile, which is launched along a fixed trajectory and cannot be recalled. The Bagua offense is more like a cruise missile, which can adjust to different weather conditions or a moving target after the launch. A poem on the secret of baguazhang states that "of the thirty-six strategies, walking away is best, since there is no need to intercept or block. This can cause the opponent's attack to fall into the void. The attack must come from the body, with the hand and foot arriving together." The "thirty-six strategies" above refer to Sun Zi's *Art of War*.

Baguazhang is especially effective against multiple attackers because of its mobility, speed, and power. A widely circulated story about Li Cunyi explains that he got his nickname "Single Saber Li" during the Boxer Rebellion, when he repeatedly led his men into battle against European soldiers armed with rifles and pistols and was so effective that his sleeves appeared dyed red. Baguazhang training includes walking on tree stumps placed in a circle and between high posts embedded in the ground to sim-ulate multiple opponents. Special palm training also enables baguazhang fighters to deliver different energetic kinds of palm strikes—crushing, vi-brating, whipping—that are used against different body types and body parts. Master Jerry Alan Johnson has chimes hanging in his training area and can sound different tones merely by striking a sandbag lying on a table fifteen feet away.

In *The Essence of Internal Martial Arts,* Master Johnson states that the internal boxer undergoes four levels of transformation—the Martial Artist, the Healer, the Scholar, and the Priest: "[The levels] specifically work with the body-mind-emotion and spirit. Each level of transformation teaches the student something unique about himself and encourages him to a higher state of enlightenment…. There are two elements at work in each level and they are in a constant state of contradiction with each other…True Self: Divine Self/Spiritual Self/Light and False Self: Ego/Primal Self/Darkness."[73]

Xingyiquan

Speculations as to the origins of xingyiquan are varied. Some believe it was created by Bodhidharma and the Shaolin Temple. Popular sentiment leans toward Yue Fei, a heroic general of the Song dynasty (960–1279). Others prefer more verifiable historical records and look to Ji Jike (1620–80) and the father of modern xingyiquan, Li Luoneng (1808–90), who taught Guo Yunshen and Liu Qilan.

Although all three internal martial arts have a technical basis in Shaolin Quan, the connection is most obvious in xingyiquan, which is linear, direct, and aggressive, with an emphasis on fist strikes. Its method of defense is attack, and it has been likened to an energetic cannonball or to the head of the dragon.

Dukes's *Bodhisattva Warriors* contains some interesting information on the origin of the word *xingyi*, although his sources are unclear. Dukes claims that *xingyi* is a translation of *samasthana*, a form of Buddhist self-awareness training. He writes: "This term, which literally means a 'configuration' or 'distinctive collective patterning or shape,' was used in the Vajramukti tradition to depict a series of practices designed to blend, intermingle and then dissolve all the various faces *(sthana)* worn by the practitioner.... [A]t its simplest level, the performance of *pratima* involved creating an internal mental drama within which students visualized, and then warded off, various kinds of armed and unarmed attacks. Later these attacks would be visualized along with appropriate emotional responses."[74]

Stories concerning Yue Fei (1103–42) abound. Although his family was poor, he was well educated by his mother and from an early age was an avid reader, with Sun Tzu's *Art of War* being among his favorites. He learned Shaolin Quan from a local man who had studied in the Shaolin Temple and at the age of nineteen joined the Song army to fight the Jin, a nomadic people who were invading China from the north. His bravery, intelligence, and honor won him rapid promotion, and within six years he was made a general and later put in command of the army fighting the Jin. He is credited with being the first to introduce a systematic wushu training program for Chinese armies. He is said to have created two forms of training. The internal style became known as xingyiquan, while the external style, which emphasized the grappling skills, became known as Eagle Claw.

Yue Fei's armies won victory after victory and pushed the Jin back north. The Jin, however, bribed the Song prime minister, Chin Kua, to recall Yue Fei and imprison him on trumped-up charges. When nothing dishonorable and no accusers could be found, he was poisoned and died in jail at the age of thirty-eight. This is regarded as one of the most infamous acts of treachery in Chinese history. Twenty years after his death, the new emperor, Xiao Zong, cleared Yue Fei's name and relocated his grave to a place of honor overlooking Hangzhou's beautiful West Lake. The emperor placed statues of Chin Kua and his wife kneeling in shame at the foot of Yue Fei's grave.

Some think Yue Fei may have learned xingyiquan in the Wudang Mountains, which border Henan Province, Yue's birthplace. They point out that Yue Fei lived at approximately the same time as taijiquan's legendary founder, Zhang Sanfeng, and in the same geographical area. Proponents of the Wudang origin also note that the theoretical basis of xingyiquan, the Five Phases, or Five Elements, theory, is closely related to taijiquan's yin-yang theory, both of which are associated with Daoism rather than Buddhism, the religion of the Shaolin tradition.

Closer to the modern era, records show that Ji Jike (1620–80) formulated and taught an internal style of boxing called *xinyiliuhequan* (heart and mind six harmonies fist), or *xinyiquan* (heart and mind fist) for short. This style was carried on in subsequent generations by teachers that included Cao Jianwu and, later, Dai Longbang (1713–1802). Li Luoneng learned xinyiquan from the Dai family and in turn created xingyiquan, which he based on the theory of Five Elements *(wu xing).*

Xingyiquan training is simple (but not easy) in the sense that it is based on just five basic movements, which reflect the Five Elements. Xingyiquan practice normally commences with *pi quan,* which can be translated as "splitting fist" and is associated with the metal element. In this movement, the hands rise up together and then pull apart as they sink down, akin to the splitting action of an ax. The pi quan resembles the overturning palm of baguazhang but tends to be applied in a more straight-ahead manner. Pi quan features the properties of rise, drill, fall, and overturn also found in baguazhang.

Each of the five (element) fists is associated with a corresponding yin organ and, if performed properly, will benefit that organ. In other words, the practice of xingyiquan is a form not only of martial training but also of health-enhancing qigong. According to Master Sun Lutang, if pi quan is performed properly, it creates "mild" qi in the lungs, which in turn will strengthen the body.

Following the generation cycle of the Five Elements, pi quan is followed by the water element fist, *zuan quan*. This is translated as the "drilling fist" and is likened to water suddenly spurting out of the ground. The striking fist drills upward in a straight line from the waist level to the head level while the other hand pulls back toward your body. It roughly resembles an uppercut but is not generated with a "hooking" action, based on the turning of the hips and waist. Proper practice of zuan quan can tonify or fill the kidneys, generating internal strength and smooth boxing skills.

Beng quan follows zuan quan. *Beng* is often interpreted as "smashing" or "crushing." Being part of the wood element, it is likened to an arrow that is shot straight and fast. Rapid contraction and expansion enables the boxer to shoot beng quan in quick and continuing succession. Correct performance makes the qi of the liver smooth, which in turn will enhance the shen (spirit) and strengthen bones and tendons.

Pao quan is the fire element and is commonly translated as "pounding." It is likened to a shell shot from a cannon. One hand wedges up and out down the center line, clearing an opponent's guard, while the other hand simultaneously strikes forward, similar to in beng quan. The fire organ is the heart. Sun Lutang writes of pao quan: "When its *qi* is mild, it makes the heart nimble and dexterous. When its *qi* is perverse, it makes the heart muddled and ignorant."

Heng quan, or "crossing fist," is associated with the spleen and the earth element. The "crossing" describes the motion of the opponent's striking fist being intercepted by the front hand while the rear hand or forearm simultaneously crosses under and attacks the ribs, armpit, or elbow. Correct performance of heng quan will keep the qi mild and the stomach and spleen at ease. In terms of the Five Elements, the earth element is associated with the center. It thus has the function of holding all the other organs in their proper, harmonious place. A weak spleen causes panic, which will in turn cause all forms to lose their proper shape.

Since these five shapes and their interaction constitute the essence of xinyiquan, traditional teachers insist that each fist be thoroughly understood and mastered before proceeding to the next. My teacher Rose Li made us practice each fist for several months before we went on to the next, and she commented that this method of teaching was a "crash course" compared to her own training. She warned that because xingyiquan is linear and uses fist striking, it is mistakenly regarded by many external martial artists as almost the same as their own arts and therefore easy to master. Its internal dynamics, she pointed out, are quite different. When I try to explain the energy of xingyiquan to my own students, I use the image of a dragon coming straight at you. Because the dragon always undulates, the up and down internal movement is emphasized; each part of your body is in continual motion, not just the arms and hands. In contrast to xingyiquan, baguazhang would be a circling dragon.

Of the three internal arts, Miss Li's favorite was xingyiquan because she considered that it saved her life. In private, she related to me that her parents were both in their forties when she was born and that she had an older sister who just seemed to sicken and then die when she was approaching the age of ten. The same thing started happening to her at the age of eight, and her well-off Beijing "mandarin" family sought all kinds of medical help, both Chinese and Western, to no avail. With some trepidation (since they regarded boxers as ruffians), they decided to follow some friends' advice and took her to a famous local xingyiquan master, Deng Yunfeng. Within a year, her fragility was transformed into robust health as she trained daily under the supervision of Master Deng, whom in time she came to regard as a second father. When Deng died, she and her wushu brothers helped financially support his family.

Once a xingyi practitioner has mastered each of the "five shapes," all five fists are practiced together in the "linking form." The linking sequence is considered the most important and fundamental form of practice in xingyiquan. Master Liang and Dr. Yang write: "You begin to understand the theory of mutual production and conquest and apply it in the applications.... You learn to unify the external manifestation (shape) and the internal mind (yi) and from this unification to build Chi to a higher level and circulate it smoothly. Through this unification you also learn how to raise up your spirit of vitality."[75]

The five shapes can also be elaborated into the practice of the Twelve Shapes, which refers to the twelve animal forms. Each animal has its own short sequence of movements, and after these are mastered they can be combined: for example, into the Eight Animal Form or the Twelve Animal Form. The spirit and the way of moving is different for each animal, although they all employ variations of the basic five fists. The twelve animals are the dragon, tiger, monkey, horse, bear, eagle, snake, hawk, chicken, water lizard, swallow, and the mythical Tai Bird.

Many modern xingyiquan practitioners also include in their training the art of *yi quan,* which was created by Master Wang Xiangzhai (1885–1963). Wang was made a lineage disciple of the famous Guo Yunshen, even though he studied with him for only five years, from the age of eight to thirteen, until Guo's death.

Wang claimed that the essence of Guo's teaching was standing meditation *(zhanzhuang)* and that Guo felt the martial artists of his day were too preoccupied with the minute details of form. Guo practiced zhanzhuang a lot while he was in prison (for killing a man with his bare hands), and it made him very strong. Wang Xiangzhai diligently followed his example, and he too developed explosive and surprising power (especially given his slight build), for which he became famous by his late twenties.

In his thirties Wang Xiangzhai spent ten years traveling through China tracing the history and practices of xingyiquan. Eventually, Wang formed his own system that he called *yi quan,* dropping all forms and concentrating on the development of the mind *(yi).* Some of his followers, especially in the Beijing area, started calling the art *dachengquan* (great achievement boxing). Although at first flattered, Wang did not approve of the name because, he reasoned, "Knowledge really has no end. How can we call it 'great achievement'? There is no finishing point."[76] The name *dachengquan* survives today.

In yi quan, eight static standing postures are used for training stillness, intent, and internal energy, which are the foundation of the system. In the later stages of yi quan practice, the practitioner takes these internal qualities into subtle physical movements, *tui shou* (push hands), and finally into *san shou* (freestyle fighting).

There is much overlap between the standing meditation practices common in Buddhism and certain yi quan postures. Having practiced both, I would say the differences are subtle but important. In yi quan, much attention is paid to the particulars of posture (see chapter 7), and the postures tend to be held for longer periods, commonly twenty minutes to an hour. This makes them much more physically demanding. The manner in which intention is used is also important. The reader is reminded that the Buddha taught two broad streams of meditation—concentration *(samadhi)* and wisdom *(pañña).*

The standing postures, as with prolonged sitting meditation, can stir up the qi and can produce shaking, sounds, voices, colors, and hallucinations that seem to come from another level of consciousness. Zen practitioners often call this *makyo,* or mind projections (although it literally means "the world of demons"). Others see it as a release of suppressed memories, emotions, and energies. I advise my students to keep on observing with "bare attention," refraining from interference. Even if these are just mind projections, they often can give you a clue as to the state and specific dynamics of your mind.

Master Wang Xiangzhai wrote:

> The standing exercise represents a very special accumulation of knowledge in China. But in the past there were very few people who paid attention to it because most people thought it was too simple. They wondered how, by sitting or standing in a single posture without moving, can you improve health?... Standing can be compared to the work of Zen: First you start with the precepts, then you cultivate wisdom, then you verify with the mind, and finally you achieve enlightenment in the void. Only when we have completed the work of understanding emptiness and the exploration of polarities, can we practice the Tao. So in this respect, the work of Zen and the work of martial arts are the same.[77]

And he traced his art back to Bodhidharma and the Five Animal Frolics: "During the Han Dynasty, Joa [Hua] Tou created the 'five animal frolics,' which are the substance of the art of standing. But during the period that followed, few people practiced the art and gradually it was lost until the middle of the Northern Dynasty, when Bodhidharma came to China from India. Bodhidharma taught his disciples the Sutras, but also techniques for strengthening their muscles and ligaments. He combined the Five Animal Frolics and the methods for changing the ligaments *(yijinjing)* and washing the bone marrow *(shi soei ching)* to create the *Yiquan* system (mind or intention boxing), also called *xinyiquan* (heart and mind boxing)."[78]

6

Why Did Bodhidharma Go Back West?

The Material Paradise

For the past five hundred years, Western science, technology, culture, and religion have been sweeping the entire planet. Today, thanks to advances in technology and to corporate concentration, American popular culture is becoming global culture. The world can experience American lifestyles in real time.

Even though Christianity remains the formal religion of the West, in many ways we have become willing converts to the subtle new religion of Scientism. We look to science and technology to miraculously save us from our self-created follies, similar to the way we once looked to human prophets and messiahs. We look to science to tell us what is "real," and in our age of quantification, this is usually determined by measurement. This works well on the physical level, but the human being and life are far more than the physical. Huston Smith observes that "modern science only requires one ontological field, the physical. Within this level it begins with matter that is perceptible, and to perceptible matter it in the end returns.... Itself occupying no more than a single ontological plane, science challenged by implication the notion that other planes exist. As its challenge was not effectively met, it swept the field...values, life meanings, purposes and qualities slip through science like sea slips through the nets of fishermen."[79]

This sweep by science has led to some absurd conclusions, not least of which is that consciousness is nothing more than electrical currents and biochemical reactions inside the brain.

In many cases, direct cause and effect cannot be presently proved because the sheer scale or complexity makes it difficult. Life is more like a giant interacting web than an accumulation of simple, linear pieces. Sometimes cause and effect are measurable, but we have not figured out what to measure, our measuring tools are not yet sufficiently developed, or it is simply not in the interest of individuals or corporations to measure it, and thus much truth remains consigned to uncertainty or unreality. It is strange, however, how quickly the unreal can gain legitimacy once there are profits to be made.

By so outwardly turning our attention in order to manipulate the physical world, we have neglected our inner development and perpetuated a dangerous psychological gap in our understanding, like that of a child who plays with a powerful weapon. History shows that we are poor at anticipating the negative side effects and consequences of new technologies. In addition, many of our timesaving innovations do not save time since technology tends to generate greater complexity. How many people today, with vastly enhanced technological capabilities, feel that they have more time on their hands than ten or twenty years ago? It is not logical to try to improve human life through self-serving market and political forces without a comprehensive study and understanding (beyond the present restrictions of the scientific model) of what it means to be human—without what Smith calls values, life meanings, purposes, or senses of innate quality.

The Challenge of the Present

As we stand at the beginning of a new millennium, we as human beings face unprecedented challenges. The way in which modern science and technology have transformed the planet within a few centuries has been nothing short of miraculous—or disastrous.

The optimists, who seem to be in the majority, are of two kinds. The true believers of Scientism downplay the negative consequences of technological society and look forward to further miracles that will not only fix our present problems but finally create the Material Paradise.

The technologies of the twenty-first century will be interrelated, generating the possibility of molecular robots, nanotechnological manipulation of DNA, robotic viruses, artificial intelligence implants, cloning, designer babies, and many other creations that most people seem to presume will remain in the realm of science fiction. Their actualization in fact may be as near as twenty or thirty years away.

The second kind of optimist looks forward to spiritual regeneration. Some believe that a New Age of spirituality is dawning and that we are merely experiencing the dark before the dawn. They point to the renewed interest in religion and spirituality, including the popularity of Eastern traditions, shamanism, New Age spirituality, and even fundamentalism in Christianity. They also point to increased global cooperation. Both kinds of optimists tend to think that raising the possibility of major human catastrophe is merely pessimism since humanity has always triumphed over adversity.

The one factor that is different from past threats, however, is the sheer scale of the problems confronting us, which is nothing less than planetary. This is a direct result of our rapid technological progress. The more we control, the more can get out of control. Global warming is increasing at the highest rate in 100 million years. More than 30,000 species of flora and fauna are dying off each year, which is the highest rate since an asteroid wiped out the dinosaurs 65 million years ago. Biologists called that the Fifth Extinction and call the present man-made phenomenon the Sixth Extinction. The first four extinctions were caused by ice ages!

For better or worse, we have created a de facto global community, which needs global cooperation in order to solve its problems. The environmental crisis we have been discussing is an obvious example as is our current obsession, terrorism. Other such problem areas include the rapidly increasing gap between the rich and poor, both within individual countries and within the community of nations; the control and monitoring of technological and scientific innovation; and the impending shortage of energy and fresh water, which is estimated to occur just before the year 2020. We can actually survive without oil, but not without water.

In order to achieve this level of cooperation, we need to transcend the greed and conflict that are presently dragging us down at so many levels—individual, corporate, religious, and national. It is common to believe that we would all be happy if only we had "more," so we look to science to give us more—but the tendency to look at life in terms of quantity rather than quality was created by science itself. The material level is only one level of our existence, and to limit ourselves to that level is retrogressive.

Moreover, if we look more carefully at our discontent we will see that our feelings of insufficiency arise from comparison with others, not from some absolute level of possessions that define the *haves* from the *have-nots*. Even "poor" people in Western countries have much more than "average" people in most poor countries, who account for the majority of the global population. But the poor in all countries, developed and undeveloped, compare themselves with the richest of the rich—because that is what they often see on TV.

Alan Watts, one of the twentieth century's most famous interpreters of Eastern spirituality, was long ago alarmed at the direction of modern society, which he felt had lost sight of mankind's true nature and destiny. Watts, a doctor of divinity, felt that Eastern religions could provide

Christians with new focus and inspiration. His *The Supreme Identity*, written in 1949, is as relevant now as then:

> Our religious and educational institutions are providing neither the wisdom nor power to cope with the political, economic, and psychological predicament in which we find ourselves. There can be little doubt that, if it follows its present course, the final result of Western man's "conquest of nature," scientific progress and cultural imperialism will be a "last state worse than the first."…
> The time has come for Christians to take the spiritual traditions of Asia seriously, to recognize that their presence among us is nothing less than providential…this does not call for any doctrinal alteration of Christianity…. Spiritual traditions such as Vedanta, Buddhism and Taoism are not religions in the strict sense, and cannot be regarded as competing with Christianity. The wisdom which Asia has to offer embodies not only the human mind's most profound understanding of life, but also a knowledge essential to human order and sanity.

An Integral Spiritual Path

As I speak to people about the need for urgent change within society, I sense a substantial amount of interest in what I have to say, but this does not seem to translate into action. I can only guess at the reasons for this— they have neither the time nor energy to pursue it; they hope things are going to somehow work out for the best; they are confused by all the different opinions and options available.

I feel that the broad legacy of the Shaolin Temple is a valuable model for human development and can close the gap between the power of our technology and our wisdom in using such power. In the first place, Buddhism and Daoism have universal appeal because they are not tied to a particular land, culture, or people. Both teachings are addressed to all human beings, explaining why we suffer and how we can liberate ourselves from suffering. They see pairs of opposites such as right/wrong and human/divine not as eternal and fixed but as fluid, interactive, and interrelated.

Certainly the number of Buddhists in the West has been rising rapidly, far in excess of the numbers of Buddhist immigrants arriving from the East. In America there were 200,000 Buddhists in 1960, 400,000 in 1990, and nearly 1,100,000 in 2001. Other estimates are as high as three to four million. In Europe, there are probably more than three million Buddhists. Many more millions practice taijiquan, although they may be unclear as to its Daoist spiritual dimensions.

Perhaps the West is destined to be the custodian of Eastern spirituality as the younger generations in the East, in a sort of yin-yang dynamic, become increasingly influenced by popular Western (i.e., American) culture, craving the same techno-toys and celebrity buzz as their counterparts in New York or Los Angeles. Thirty years ago in India and Singapore, and more recently in China, the locals were truly puzzled as to why I, with a Western passport and qualification as a chartered accountant, would be roaming their country asking about old-fashioned spirituality and martial arts.

The *Dao De Jing* states:

> Weapons, being instruments of ill omen, are not the tools of the cultured, who use them only when unavoidable....
> Good warriors do not harm, good fighters don't get mad, good winners don't contend, good employers serve their workers. This is called the virtue of noncontention; this is called mating with the supremely natural and pristine.

In addition to their lofty teachings about the cruelty and stupidity of war, history attests to that fact that the followers of Daoism and Buddhism have in fact been remarkably free of violence and war throughout the ages, being spread by teachers rather than armies. Indeed, Buddhism has survived widespread persecution without resorting to retaliation. One of the most devastating blows suffered by Buddhism was its annihilation in northern India by the Muslims during the twelfth century. During the twentieth century, Buddhism has come under severe attack by Pol Pot and the Khmer Rouge in Cambodia and, at various times, by the Communist Party in China.

Another reason Buddhist-Daoist spirituality is particularly appropriate to our times lies in its straightforward, down-to-earth, and logical explanation of Perennial Wisdom. The teaching is not hidden in symbols, imagery, obscure texts, or ritual but explains, in cause-and-effect terms, the consequences of our actions. This causality, however, is not to be understood by studying books or conducting experiments in the lab; it must be seen and experienced internally. Buddhist-Daoist spirituality directly challenges each and every one of us to look immediately and directly into our own nature, which takes a skill not widely taught at present.

The notion that our thoughts, emotions, and actions may be conditioned by past events and by our external environment has become more familiar if not completely accepted. Physics teaches us the fact of conditionality from a different perspective. Even the densest physical matter is not solid, but is made up mostly of empty space and minute particles that are in constant motion. Fritjof Capra writes, "The basic oneness of the universe is not only the central characteristic of the mystical experience, but is also one of the most important revelations of modern physics.... The constituents of matter and the basic phenomena involving them are all interconnected, interrelated and interdependent; that they cannot be understood as isolated entities, but only as integrated parts of the whole."[80]

The foundations of a modern Buddhist-Daoist system must consist of a basic moral code of nonharming plus a meditation practice aimed at self-inquiry and wisdom. Probably the most accessible and practical form of Buddhist meditation currently available to Western laypeople is vipassana. This form of meditation is based on the Buddha's Sutra on the Foundations of Mindfulness *(Satipatthana Sutta)* and owes its present popularity to a twentieth-century revival in Burma, led by Mahasi Sayadaw and U Ba Khin. This new wave of vipassana has been spread mainly by lay teachers and seeks to go back to the roots of Buddhist meditation, elevating personal insight and experience over monastic tradition. Its teachers, freed from traditional restrictions, have explored various ways of making the practice more intelligible and available to the West. One teacher who has been particularly successful in this respect is Jon Kabat-Zinn, who became famous for using mindfulness meditation to treat chronic pain and stress-related disorders in his Stress Reduction Clinic at the University of Massachusetts Medical Center.

Stephen Batchelor writes that the vipassana revival "has led to the impression that some Buddhists practice vipassana, while others (such as practitioners of Zen or Tibetan Buddhism) do not. In fact, vipassana is central to all forms of Buddhist meditation practice. The distinctive goal of any Buddhist contemplative tradition is a state in which inner calm *(samatha)* is unified with insight *(vipassana)*. Over the centuries, each tradition has developed its own methods for actualizing this state."[81]

I do not think it would be outrageous to compare elements of this current vipassana revival to the early days of Chan, when emphasis was placed on the immediateness of prajna as the key element to enlightenment. In the early days of Chan, book learning, intellectual discussion, and "external paraphernalia" were cast aside; ordinary everyday life, directness, and simplicity were emphasized.

There is a body of opinion that would agree with the modern Zen master Seung Sahn when he describes Zen as a "marriage between vipassana-style Indian meditation and Chinese Taoism."[82] If this is indeed true, then is it not possible to recreate some of the original Shaolin Temple "magic" by combining a modern, stripped-down vipassana with a modern Chinese Taoism, in the form of qigong and the Chinese internal martial arts? Together, as has been explained in earlier chapters, they would comprise a comprehensive mind-body spiritual system in the Ageless Wisdom tradition. Moreover, this system would be the product of hundreds of years of testing, refinement, and integration rather than an arbitrary, eclectic collection of disciplines.

The Three Regulations found in qigong and the Chinese internal martial arts cover the body, or physical postures; the breath, together with the control of qi; and the mind, which includes the emotions, the intellectual mind, and the higher mind. In this system, as we have seen, Regulation of the Body would include Western-style aerobic, stretching, and strength-building exercises plus exercises that are similar to the currently popular hatha yoga. It would also include self-massage, healing sounds to treat specific internal conditions, and attention to food intake, balanced according to yin-yang principles. The latter would be similar to what is known in the West as macrobiotics.

Regulation of Breathing, next, would cover much of the same ground as pranayama and kundalini yoga, as well as the Western stress-reduction techniques that these disciplines have inspired. In addition, advanced qigong practitioners are able to draw energy from the external environment (from the earth and heavens) and circulate it through the channels, meridians, and organs for a wide variety of purposes including mind-body health, tantra, and internal alchemy.

Regulation of the Mind, finally, would include the spiritual transformational elements covered by Hindu, Buddhist, and Daoist meditation traditions, visualization to direct the qi, and unraveling of emotional and energetic blocks, as covered by modern psychotherapy, bioenergetics, and the like.

If the above seems like too much to learn or too good to be true, it must be remembered that a transformed consciousness brings with it far more integration and simplicity than we normally experience. It would be a very natural integration, whereas the scientific, analytical approach breaks life down into ever smaller conceptual pieces, which become overwhelming in their profusion and conflicting needs. In reality, all parts are interrelated and interdependent. Body, emotions, and mind do not ever exist separately. With a little knowledge and skill, it is possible to turn normal physical activities into qigong exercises that also work with qi and the mind.

Another aspect of this kind of effortless confluence lies in the fact that when one knows oneself, from the inside, then one also knows others because our deep dynamics are the same. The *Dao De Jing* advised: "They know the world without even going out the door. They see the sky and its pattern without even looking out the window. The further out it goes, the less knowledge is; therefore sages know without going, name without seeing, complete without striving."[83]

Once we have developed skills, or gongfu, in qigong self-regulation techniques, it would be natural and easy to apply them in all areas of life, similar to way we would benefit from going to posture classes or embarking on a physical workout program. The Chinese, as we have seen, used qigong for spiritual transformation, health, and healing and in the martial arts. Medical qigong therapy is one of the main branches of traditional Chinese medicine, which is gaining rapid acceptance in the West. With some knowledge of traditional Chinese medicine, one could treat oneself in a similar manner to a Chinese doctor, or indeed, with extra training, one could treat others through qi projection and the prescription of qigong self-regulation exercises, even for serious illnesses.

Within Buddhism, there is an ongoing bias against psychic or supernatural powers, which are known as *siddhi* and may arise at certain stages of meditative skill. In fact, they are listed among the obstacles to enlightenment, which, it should be noted, also include such items as home, family, activities, traveling, and study. It is thought that psychic powers, being extraordinary, are liable to trap us through pride or seduce us into becoming attached to them. From my personal point of view, I see the ability to sense and project qi as something natural—not supernatural. Some are carried away by it, some are not. It would seem that the trap is attachment, whether we are talking about siddhi, maintaining tradition, playing a musical instrument, acquiring knowledge of any sort, or upholding moral precepts. All life is conditioned and part of the oneness.

Martial arts training has much potential because it can be a powerful mind-body exercise even while it teaches us how to handle emotions, ego and the threats from predators, bullies, or those out of control or balance. This is yet another example of how integrated training can save us time while yielding superior results. That having been said, the end product of this training will depend on what is being taught and who is teaching it.

Many presentations of Eastern martial arts talk about spirituality, but few deliver anything substantial, mostly paying lip service to respect, non-violence, and the ability to "focus" and "center." Some sit quietly in "meditation" for five minutes after a practice session.

The internal martial arts, if properly taught, can be a comprehensive and integrated path of the warrior, healer, and sage. This is possible because the fighting arts, psychophysical exercises, healing techniques, and transformational philosophy are all based on yin-yang and Five Elements theory. Whatever you do, you embody the yin-yang symbol, seeking balance in all circumstances, whether negotiating the emotional currents of intimate relationships or the raw fury of a physical attack. In this respect, taijiquan push-hands skill is invaluable.

As we have seen, emptiness *(wuji)* underlies the interplay of yin and yang *(taiji)*. The Taiji Classics tell us:

> Taiji is born of Wuji. It is the origin of dynamic and static states
> and the mother of yin and yang. If they move, they separate. If
> they remain static, they combine.

If you really want to master the martial techniques of taijiquan, therefore, you have to be empty, and in order to be empty, you have to do what is essentially spiritual work, letting go of ego with all its fears, desires, and attachments.

It should be pointed out that qigong and the internal martial arts provide ample opportunity for those who want to practice absorption or concentration meditation in addition to vipassana. Various forms of sitting and standing meditation—for example, those used in yi quan—are part and parcel of these disciplines.

Impact on Culture and Society

Some secularists find it difficult to see how spirituality can solve our real-life problems, while some engaged in spiritual pursuits feel that secular matters are beneath them. In fact, the individual and collective, the inner and outer, the subjective and objective, the religious and secular are all interrelated in precisely the manner that yin-yang theory explains.

Individual self-transformation affects society and culture because we become more aware, sensitive, and compassionate and therefore perceive a far greater range of cause and effect and interrelatedness. We then act more cooperatively and compassionately, not because some authority figure tells us we should, but because we see for ourselves subtle causes and effects. We will perhaps be reminded of Vivekananda's words: "There is no supernatural, says the yogi, but there are in nature gross manifestations and subtle manifestations. The subtle are the causes, the gross are the effects."[84]

These effects of self-transformation do not depend on the attainment of "full enlightenment." Even a modest change in consciousness, a modest widening of view will make us truly capable of a global perspective, rather than just talking about it as an ideal. We will begin to realize that our physical body does not describe the boundaries of our "self" or "I." Given that the world's population is now more than six billion, a slight shift in consciousness will have a vastly more powerful effect than any new technological or scientific miracle. Imagine a six-billion-times increase in ongoing trust, caring, sharing, sensitivity, and responsibility.

The most immediate effects of a shift in consciousness will be reflected in what we buy and whom we elect to power. When we realize that we are interrelated and interdependent with others on this planet, we will no longer embrace a culture that consumes and throws away just to pass the time. We can, for example, demand cars (and other forms of transport) that last longer, consume less fuel, and do not damage the environment. We can stop treating the air, land, and oceans as garbage dumps, for we will realize that we are what we breathe, eat, and drink.

Taking greater care of the planet means taking greater care of all people, not only those that are an extension of our personal ego and identity, based on country, race, or religion. When one area is diseased, whether physically, militarily, economically, or ideologically, it is difficult to contain the spread without a cooperative effort.

As we individually develop an evolved sense of cause and effect and interconnectedness, we can expect to see it grow in political parties, in the judicial system, in corporations, in the media. We will not be so easily swayed by appearance and charm, will not so lightly excuse corruption and deceit, will not stray from the course of meaningful change, even if it requires long-term commitment.

At the moment, scientific and technological innovators, largely motivated by profit, are allowed to get away with minimal testing on the grounds that the technology is new and nothing can be conclusively proved harmful. When things go wrong, which happens with regularity, the innovators are rarely made to pay the true costs. If they are corporations, they can make a token payoff to desperate individuals or, in a worst-case scenario, declare bankruptcy and then reform themselves into other corporations. The end result of all this is that ordinary people are paying the costs of the "free market" in the form of disease, degradation, and death. The profit is reaped by the few (mostly large corporations) while the costs

are borne by the many—a dynamic that reinforces our deliberate eco-
nomic policies of rewarding the rich in the hope that their entrepreneurial
efforts will trickle down and raise the poor. To me, it seems unwise to
build a society on a foundation of greed, manipulation, and inequality.
All of this does not happen by bad luck but by design. The invisible hand
of the market is not really invisible. We now have computers to track it,
even through the deliberately confusing maze of corporate complexity.
When a society of ordinary people come to collective clarity (through
personal clarity), they will also fashion the will to be heard and heeded.

When we understand our internal dynamics a bit better we will see
that the seemingly strange things the Buddha and the physicists are
telling us are true. The subject (the "I") is not really confined inside our
skin and the object is not a fixed thing out there, since they depend on
and interact with each other. The Buddha long ago pointed out that all
things, including human beings, are interdependent. Rapid advances in
communications technology have made the interdependence of subject
and object much more obvious. TV viewers can vote to determine the
outcome of certain shows; by clicking their remotes, they can decide
which programs are popular and which are not. So far, so good. Democracy
seems to be working and the masses are in control. What viewers do not
seem to realize, however, is that they are controlled by the media at least
as much as they control the media.

Once we become aware of our own internal dynamics, we will also
realize the importance of what we take into ourselves—sound and visual
images as well as air, water, and food. We will simultaneously understand
how our own words, actions, and even thoughts affect others. It will then
be natural to share this knowledge with our children and see it reflected
in formal education and throughout the media and entertainment indus-
tries, and the rest of the world.

Section III:
Practices

Instructions for Practical Exercises

Wuji Posture

One of the most important physical postures used in qigong, taijiquan, yi quan and the other internal martial arts is the basic wuji (emptiness) standing posture. Since this posture relaxes and aligns the body in order to promote the regulation and circulation of qi, it is helpful in any activity involving standing, walking, and sitting. My personal experience is that the principles of wuji posture significantly enhance Buddhist sitting, standing, and walking meditation practices since the body is stable, relaxed, and in correct posture. It also helps in a wide range of everyday activities such as desk work, manual labor, and sports. Here is a brief description of the wuji posture.

The first rule is to stand with the feet flat on the ground, parallel, and shoulders' width apart. The weight is evenly distributed between the feet, and held just in front of your heels.

Now check your posture. Start from the top of the head and work downward. "Suspend" the head: imagine that the head is suspended from above by an invisible string. This gently stretches the spine. The specific part of the head being suspended is the *baihui* (acupuncture) point, which is toward the back of the head, midway between the apex of each ear. Your chin is slightly tucked in, with your gaze just below the horizontal; the neck is slightly elongated but open, not tight.

Gently touch your tongue to your upper palate. This may cause increased saliva, which is regarded as valuable and thus must be conserved by swallowing. Touching the tongue to the roof of the mouth also connects the Governing Vessel, which runs up the back of the body, to the Conception Vessel, which runs down the front.

Lower and relax the shoulders and chest while stretching your back. The chest is slightly hollow and concave, while the back of the body is convex and the scapulae are separated. (This is consonant with the yin-yang notion that the front of the body is yin and the back, yang.) Note that this rule does not recommend a slumping or slouching posture since the head and spine are erect. This posture allows the qi to sink to the abdomen (or more specifically, the dantian), keeping you relaxed and giving you a wider mental perspective. Stress generally does the opposite: raises the shoulders, makes the breathing shallow, and creates the feeling of being hunched and hemmed in.

Hollow the armpits, drop the elbows, and relax the wrists. The armpits are hollowed by rotating the hands at the sides of the body to face backward. The armpits should open slightly so that they could hold an egg. The elbows and wrists relax but feel as if they are being pulled toward the ground. The palms are hollow and the fingers are curved naturally but are "open," not tight and rigid.

Relax the waist and hips, tighten the anal sphincter, rounding the perineal area, and bend the knees. Imagine the waist and the hips relaxing and sinking into the legs, then the knees bending so that the weight sinks or drains into the ground. At the same time, the buttocks tuck under slightly, as if the coccyx were being pulled down by a weight. This posture should cause the small of the back to flatten out, and for a bend to form at the junction of the torso and thighs, which is sometimes described as relaxing or folding the *kua* (inguinal area). The abdomen is relaxed as the qi sinks to the lower dantian, which is an energy reservoir located within the body below the navel.

Your state of mind will depend on the purpose of your wuji posture, but there is always awareness of your body in each moment. Generally, closed eyes will turn your attention more inward and will induce a more passive yin state, which is good for tonifying energy deficiencies. Open eyes create a more active, yang state and direct the energy outward, dispersing or projecting it.

In a sitting position, whether on a meditation cushion or on a chair, the wuji posture rules still apply except for those relevant to the legs. On a chair, the feet should be flat on the ground with the thighs horizontal; do not lean on the back of the chair. On a cushion, the outside of the crossed legs should provide a stable base on the ground, so that the body does not rock or sway. If the legs are not flexible enough for the knees to reach the ground, they may be supported by cushions.

Walking instructions follow.

Taijiquan Walking

Several western studies have found that the practice of taijiquan is one of the most effective means of improving balance in seniors and consequently reducing the incidence of falling. In fact, people of all ages can benefit from proper walking since an improper gait and posture can adversely affect the joints, spine, breathing, and much more over time. Most of us have never been taught how to walk properly.

In addition to its physical and mechanical benefits, walking as practiced in taijiquan is also a qigong exercise, pumping energy through the body by stimulating the *yongquan* acupuncture point, which is located just inside the ball of the foot.

It is easy to incorporate the principles of taijiquan and qigong walking into traditional Buddhist mindful slow walking.

1. Start from a standing posture, checking all the principles of the wuji posture.

2. Shift the weight to (say) the left leg, keeping it slightly bent at the knees. This movement should feel like filling the left and emptying the right. It is important to remember that as you shift the weight, whether side to side or back to front, the torso is maintained in an upright position, with the head as if suspended by a string.

3. When the right leg is empty, lift it, keeping it relaxed. Start inhaling as you lift. As you breathe the chest and shoulders stay relaxed.

4. Extend the right leg, touching the ground lightly with your right heel. Make sure that as you extend yout right heel the right knee joint does not lock.

5. Slowly put weight on to the right foot, feeling it roll forward from the heel towards the front of your foot. Exhale as your foot rolls on to the ground. This is a careful, fluid catlike step, which causes your torso, still upright, to move forward. Make sure that the knees bend in the same direction as the feet, otherwise you will feel wobbly and a twisting of the joints. All the while the eyes look ahead, not at the ground, which would cause a curvature of the spine and a feeling of being pulled forward.

6. Keep transferring your weight onto the right leg, emptying the left. When it is empty, lift it as in #3 and keep walking.

As you walk, the lower part of the body should feel stable and rooted, while the upper body is light and relaxed. When you get accustomed to the slow walking as above, you can use it at normal speeds. This kind of walking is especially helpful on slippery or uneven ground since the heel touches lightly before weight is committed rather than being flung forward.

Yi Quan Standing Meditation

In the beginning stages, just pay "bare attention" (as in vipassana) to your body in its standing posture.

1. Start in wuji posture for several minutes, building up your standing time as you practice.

2. Move to Embracing the Post posture. Slowly move your arms up to the level of your chest as if embracing a big ball or tree trunk. The shoulders, chest, arms and fingers are all relaxed, with the palms facing in towards the chest. Avoid sharp bends at the wrists and elbows. Try to build up the length of time that you can hold this posture. If you encounter shaking, relax and make sure your posture is correct and your breathing is natural.

3. Slowly lower your arms and end in the wuji posture.

It should be noted that Embracing the Post is only one of several different postures in the yi quan system and the above instructions describe only one way of practicing the postures.

The Microcosmic Orbit

Probably the simplest and most dependable way of connecting up your microcosmic orbit is by paying attention to specific spots located on the orbit, one by one. In qigong, it is said that the yi leads the qi. Your qi will be lead through your microcosmic orbit as you pay attention to each successive acupuncture point as described below. Keep your attention to one spot until you can feel it precisely and can feel subtle sensations like tingling, heat, or cold. Then you can move on to the next point. Remember to keep the anal sphincter closed and the tongue touching the roof of the mouth. This practice can be done standing or sitting, either on a cushion or a chair.

1. Qihai, which is associated with the lower dantian. This point is located about one and a half inches below the navel, below the surface of the skin, inside the body.

2. Guanyuan. This is about three inches below the navel. In men this is near the prostate gland, and in women it is the mid point between the ovaries.

3. Huiyin. This point is at the very bottom of the torso, in the center of the perineum.

4. Changqiang. Between the tip of the coccyx and the anus.

5. Mingmen. This important qigong point is located on the spine, opposite the navel, in the small of the back, between the 2nd and 3rd lumbar vertebrae.

6. Jizhong. Below the 11th thoracic vertebra, between the adrenal glands.

7. Shendao. Between the shoulder blades, at the 5th thoracic vertebra.

8. Fengfu. In the hollow at the base of the skull.

9. Baihui. The midpoint of the line connecting the apex of the ears at the top of the head.

10. Yintang. The Third Eye, between the eyebrows.

11. Shanzhong. At the center of chest between the nipples.

12. Juque. Solar plexus.

13. Qihai.

When the microcosmic orbit is opened up, you can lead the qi from the qihai up your spine on the exhalation and down the front of the body on the inhalation, ending up back at the qihai.

Vipassana Meditation

Vipassana is based on the Buddha's *Satipatthana Sutta,* which may be translated as Discourse on the Foundations of Mindfulness. There are four broad objects of mindfulness: the body, feelings, state of mind, and mind objects. The body is the most commonly used object of mindfulness, since it is tangible and apparent. Experienced practitioners may at times find it appropriate to use feelings, state of mind, or mind objects as the object of their meditation practice.

The twentieth-century revival of vipassana, especially among lay meditators, originated in Burma and has given rise to two slightly different forms of practice. The method popularized by U Ba Khin, and subsequently by Goenka, starts by noticing the sensation of the breath as it enters the nose and follows it through the body. In this method, the meditator also systematically "sweeps" the entire body to observe subtle sensations. The description of practice offered hereunder comes from the teachings of Mahasi Sayadaw, who recommended focusing on the sensation of the breath as it rises and falls in the abdomen and mentally noting whatever occurs in the field of awareness.

It is helpful to have "clear comprehension of purpose" when you meditate, which in this case is paying "bare attention" to whatever is taking place in the field of awareness. The purpose is not to become peaceful, holy, stress free, loving, or enlightened, although such changes may in time occur. I sometimes describe the practice as spending time with yourself for no reason whatsoever. If you are happy with yourself as you are, the chances are that you will be at ease in relationship with others. As part of this clear comprehension, set aside a regular time for your formal meditation (early mornings are often most convenient) in a quiet, clean space.

This has the advantage of being non-action, no manipulation.

The next step I recommend is to check your sitting posture. Qigong's instructions on "regulation of the body" are most helpful here. See the description of wuji posture on pages 159–161. To help relaxation, put an imaginary energy ball or smile on the top of your head and feel it slowly melting down through your body like warm oil, relaxing you and washing away stress and negativity.

Next bring your attention to your abdomen, noting the physical sensations caused by the breath rising and falling. You do not have to imagine, control, adjust, or count the breath, just feel the physical sensations, which is different from thinking about the breath. Most beginners cannot do this for more than a few seconds at a time since the mind is so accustomed to activity and stimulation. It wants to be elsewhere in space and time; it wants to judge, compare, and control; it wants to concoct schemes and dreams.

When you realize that your mind has strayed, note where it is, let go, and start over again. Do not use force to try to coerce the mind or it will react. This simple practice is profound because it not only makes the mind more alert and aware, it helps us to be in the moment—here and now—and to let go of the past, whether seconds ago or years ago. The duration of the sitting meditation should be at least twenty minutes, but an hour is not unusual.

For the beginner, the instructions above are all you need. The practice is simple but it is profound and not easy. It is important to remember that the thoughts of the meditator, including judging whether vipassana is a worthwhile practice, should also be noted as part of the activity rising and falling in the field of awareness.

At times, certain objects may force themselves consistently into your awareness. Physical pain resulting from sitting still is quite common, as is past trauma or emotional pain. If noting and going back to the abdomen does not work, the meditator may choose to make the physical or emotional pain the object of observation (without analysis, internal dialogue, etc.) The thought, "It is silly to deliberately make myself uncomfortable," should itself be brought into mindfulness. This seemingly innocuous conclusion goes very deep to fundamental issues, which include pain and pleasure, the opposites, and the nature of the "I" drawing such conclusions. In terms of past emotional trauma, I feel that in most cases the skillful practice of vipassana (sometimes with qigong) can release such trauma, without any additional help from psychotherapists or psychologists. This is not to say that psychotherapists cannot help meditators, since each case is quite specific and depends on precisely what is taking place during the "meditation."

I am not of the opinion that other meditation practices including concentration, samatha, visualizing, and qigong detract from vipassana, as long as these are not done during vipassana meditation to make the sitting more interesting or to obtain "higher" states. I see this again as a matter of "clear comprehension of purpose" and of harmonizing the yin and the yang in terms of finite-infinite, active-passive, body-mind, nirvana-samsara, and the like, all the while bearing in mind that yin and yang are the same in source and essence.

A less intense form of body mindfulness, suitable for everyday activity, is noting your body's every change in posture: sitting, standing, walking, running, reclining, kneeling, and lying.

Conclusion

From my personal experience, I have no doubt that the Chan/Zen and martial arts traditions of the Song Shan Shaolin Temple are meaningfully related—and further that their intermixture has yielded extremely powerful mind-body techniques that are useful in both spiritual practice and daily life. But there are more objective reasons for considering such an assertion. If we examine Chinese history, we will find that many elements now overwhelmingly associated with the no-nonsense approach of Zen are also to be found in philosophical Daoism, which predates Bodhidharma by approximately eight hundred to one thousand years. Daoism in turn is based on much older Chinese concepts like qi and yin-yang theory, the origins of which are hidden in the mists of China's legendary period.

The concept of using martial arts for personal cultivation, qigong/dao yin exercises based on animal movements, and traditional Chinese medicine were likewise all established in China not only before Bodhidharma but even before Buddhism itself made its way along the Silk Road from India. When the powerful metaphysical insights and spiritual practices of Indian Mahayana Buddhism were scattered on this extremely fertile Chinese ground, it is not surprising that something very special bloomed.

It is important to keep in mind, as we try to examine the significance of the early days of Shaolin, that Zen and the eastern martial arts first came to the West through Japan, and consequently much Western examination of these matters is still conducted through a Japanese cultural and philosophical lens. Indeed, as we have seen, much of that lens is specifically samurai in orientation since as Esai and Dogen were bringing Zen to Japan in the twelfth century the first shoguns were coming to power. Their warrior class, the samurai, adopted Zen as their religion, and the shoguns and samurai would go on to rule and mold Japan for an astonishing seven hundred years.

In the West, there is a common assumption (which I myself used to make) that nothing of much philosophical or spiritual consequence took place in China after the Chan lineage passed to Japan. This is probably due to the lack of authoritative literature on the subject, which may in turn be a reflection of modern academia's ongoing discomfort with concepts like qi and prana.

In fact, toward the end of the first millennium C.E., Chinese philosophers began consciously combining the highest elements of Confucianism, Daoism, and Buddhism to form Neo-Confucianism, of which Fung Yu-lan writes:

> Neo-Confucianism is indeed the continuation of the idealistic wing of ancient Confucianism, and especially of the mystic tendency of Mencius. That is the reason why these men have been known as the *Tao hseuh chia* and their philosophy as the *Tao hsueh*, i.e., The Study of the Tao or Truth....
>
> The second is Buddhism, together with Taoism via the medium of Ch'anism, for of all the schools of Buddhism, Ch'anism was the most influential at the time of the formation of Neo-Confucianism.... In one sense Neo-Confucianism may be said to be the logical development of Ch'anism. Finally the third is the Taoist religion, of which the cosmological views of the Yin-Yang School formed an important element.[85]

If the learned Fung Yu-lan is right about Neo-Confucianism being the logical development of Chan, then the Neo-Confucian *taiji* ("The Supreme Ultimate") philosophy may be regarded as a spiritual legacy of the Shaolin Temple. As we have seen, taiji philosophy was subsequently used as a basis for modern qigong and the internal martial arts, manifesting the philosophy in a system of practical and comprehensive mind-body spiritual techniques. The creators and major teachers of the internal martial arts systems, which are popularly regarded as Daoist rather than Buddhist, have openly acknowledged a debt of gratitude to the genius of the early Shaolin masters.

I think of qigong and the internal martial arts as the softer, more pliable yin legacy of the Shaolin temple, in contrast to the more famous and forceful yang legacy, which includes Zen and the "external" martial arts of Shaolin, together with their many offspring, both in China and the rest of the Far East. The essence and goals of these two are the same but the means differ. Within the qigong and internal martial arts stream, it is important to remember that the ultimate goal of "mind regulation" is enlightenment and "return to the Dao." For this, surrender is unavoidable and an enlightenment practice necessary. In this book, I have suggested vipassana as an enlightenment practice that would fit in seamlessly with qigong and the internal martial arts and at the same time recall the urgency for enlightenment for which Chan is famous. Prajna, or insightful wisdom, is an important element in both Chan and vipassana.

Whether yin or yang, heart or head, enlightenment practices are desperately needed within modern society to give us direction and purpose beyond consumerism and brute force. More science and technology will not do this. Many people seem to sense that something is wrong but are overwhelmed by the stress, complexity, and competition of modern life and the lack of an alternative model of being. Confusion is a major characteristic of postmodernism. This situation reminds me of D.T. Suzuki's commentary on the first ox-herding picture: "We have contrived against our inmost nature. She is lost, for we have ourselves been led out of the way through the deluding senses. The home is growing farther away, and the byways and crossways are ever confusing. Desire for gain and fear of loss burn like fire, ideas of right and wrong shoot up like a phalanx."[86]

I think that qigong and the internal martial arts can provide us with an alternative model of being most appropriate to our current environment. They recognize that continuous change is an inescapable fact of life and therefore teach flexibility and adaptation; they recognize that the body, qi, emotions, mind, and spirit are all integrated and give us specific tools to explore their integration; they do not require a specific culture, a controlled environment (like a monastery), or subscription to a belief system; they explore the dynamics of conflict and harmony on many levels, including the physical; they include the whole being, including sexuality and emotions, as part of spiritual practice; they recognize the oneness and the emptiness underlying all beings. Furthermore, these systems have been honed and tested over many centuries and possess an internal consistency based on a sophisticated understanding of yin-yang theory.

This spiritual legacy is ideal for our times. It acknowledges the continual change and conditionality of the universe. It is direct and scientific in the ways it helps us explore and understand our inner dynamics. And it teaches us how to be present, empty, centered, sensitive, aware, and balanced so that we can ride the continual and often surprising waves of life.

The infinite reality is a single whole,
Always present in daily activities;
Creation after creation,
Transformation after transformation,
Hundreds and thousands of workings—
None of them are beyond
This present mortal being.

—*The thirteenth-century Daoist* Book of Balance and Harmony

Notes

[ACK] "The best female internal boxer": Robert W. Smith, *Martial Musings: A Portrayal of Martial Arts in the 20th Century*. Erie, Penn.: Via Media Publishing, 1999. pp. 250–257.

1   "most dangerous promise of technology": John Naisbitt, *High Tech, High Touch*. New York: Broadway Books, 1999. p. 45.

2   "Trungpa and Dhiravamsa emanate serene cheerfulness": Anne Bancroft, *Twentieth-Century Mystics and Sages*. London: Arkana Books, 1989. p. 198.

3   "In a culture intoxicated": George Leonard and Michael Murphy, *The Life We Are Given: A Long-Term Program for Realizing the Potential of Body, Mind, Heart and Soul*. New York: G.P. Putnam's Sons, 1995. p. 8. This book describes a comprehensive system of self-transformation put together by Leonard and Murphy, two pioneers of the Human Potential Movement.

4   "The master first stayed": D.T. Suzuki, *Essays in Zen Buddhism, First Series*. London: Rider and Company, 1973. p. 185.

5   "Empty-hand fighting techniques": Donn F. Draeger and Robert W. Smith, *Asian Fighting Arts*. New York: Berkley Publishing Corporation, 1974. p. 73. Smith has written a number of books on the Asian martial arts, starting in the 1960s. He was one of the first authoritative English-language authors on this subject.

6   "external paraphernalia which the intellect": Suzuki, *Essays in Zen Buddhism, Third Series*. London: Rider and Company, 1973. p. 376.

7   "Samadhi in its general characteristic": Paravahera Vajiranana Mahathera, Ph.D., *Buddhist Meditation in Theory and Practice: A General Exposition according to the Pali Canon of the Theravada School*. Kuala Lumpur: Buddhist Missionary Society, 1975. p. 43.

8   "Zen abhors anything coming between": Suzuki, *Essays in Zen Buddhism, First Series*. London: Rider and Company, 1973. p. 19.

9   "Stories linking Bodhidharma": Andy Ferguson, *Zen's Chinese Heritage*. Boston: Wisdom Publications, 2000. p. 18.

10 "In the thirteenth year": ibid., p. 27.

11 "Hui-neng is a central figure": Thomas Cleary, *Classics of Buddhism and Zen. Volume Three*. Boston and London: Shambhala Publications, 2001. p. 5.

12 "leveling of more than 4,600 monasteries": Joseph Campbell, *The Masks of God: Oriental Mythology*. New York: Penguin Books, 1976. p. 444.

13 "Zen Buddhism is the product": Suzuki, *Essays in Zen Buddhism, First Series*. London: Rider and Company, 1973. p. 163.

14 "he wanted his disciples": Fung Yu-lan, *A Short History of Chinese Philosophy*, edited by. Derk Bodde. New York: The Free Press, 1966. p. 40. Fung's work is especially helpful because it is a scholarly work written from the perspective of someone born and raised in China.

15 "a feeling of humanity towards others": Huston Smith, *The World's Religions*. San Francisco: Harper Collins, 1991. p. 172.

16 "I must emphasize the distinction": Fung Yu-lan, *A Short History of Chinese Philosophy*, edited by Derk Bodde. New York: The Free Press, 1966. p. 211.

17 "A Way can be a guide": *The Taoist Classics: The Collected Translations of Thomas Cleary, Volume One*. Boston: Shambhala Publications, 1999. Quotations from the *Dao De Jing* below are from this edition.

18 "For the West, the possibility": Campbell, *The Masks of God: Oriental Mythology*. New York: Penguin Books, 1976. pp. 6–7.

19 "Laozi despised such Confucian virtues": Fung, *Short History*, p. 101.

20 "As long as we stay with relativity": D.T. Suzuki, *Essays in Zen Buddhism, Third Series*. London: Rider and Company, 1973. p. 263.

21 "Chinese elaboration of the Doctrine of Enlightenment": see the epigraph to this chapter.

22 "The extent of the mind is so vast": *Classics of Buddhism and Zen: The Collected Translations of Thomas Cleary, Volume Three*. Boston and London: Shambhala Publications, 2001. p. 19.

23 "so-called lost people": Cleary, *The Taoist Classics*, p. 101.

24 "the way to God through psychophysical exercises": Smith, *The World's Religions*, p. 41.

25 "Surrender can take effect": *The Spiritual Teaching of Ramana Maharshi*, Berkeley and London: Shambhala Publications, 1972. pp. 66–67.

26 "the identification of the Self": Alan Watts, *The Supreme Identity: An Essay on Oriental Metaphysic and the Christian Religion*. London: Wildwood House, 1973. p. 175. This is one of the most interesting of Watts's books. Written in 1949, when Watts was thinking of leaving the priesthood, it was intended for theologians and students of comparative religion. It seems as relevant today as fifty years ago.

27 "it involves a considerable degree": ibid., pp. 175–176.

28 "It is not the result": Chogyam Trungpa, *Meditation in Action*. London: Watkins, 1974. pp. 52–56.

29 "Arguing that affairs of the spirit": Smith, *The World's Religions*, p. 42.

30 "For thousands of years": Vivekananda, *The Yogas and Other Works*. New York: Ramakrishna-Vivekananda Center, 1996. p. 577.

31 "the infinite, omnipresent manifesting power": ibid., p. 592.

32 "When one has so intensified the power of dhyana": ibid., pp. 616–617.

33 "Enlightenment, often seen as a difficult process": Katherine Anne Harper and Robert L. Brown, eds., *The Roots of Tantra*. Albany: State University of New York Press, 2002. p. 3.

34 "The ideological aspect": Andre Padoux, *The Roots of Tantra*, p. 19.

35 "It is important to recognize clearly": Jeffrey Hopkins, *The Tantric Distinction: A Buddhist's Reflections on Compassion and Emptiness*. Boston: Wisdom Publications, 1999. p. 126.
36 "While the basic teaching of Mahayana Buddhism": Chogyam Trungpa, *Cutting through Spiritual Materialism*. Berkeley: Shambhala Publications, 1973. pp. 218, 220.
37 "a powerful and potentially dangerous": Nagaboshi (Dukes), *Bodhisattva Warriors*, p. 202.
38 "much of what we know concerning *nata*": ibid., p. 174.
39 "It was probably these same secular people": ibid., p. 216.
40 "warrior-trained monks": ibid., p. 194.
41 "Taoism was only organized": ibid., p. 120.
42 "Newly developing Taoism": ibid., p. 216.
43 "Unfortunately the early Taoist healers": ibid., p. 121.
44 "The concept of holistic Wushu": Kang Gewu, *The Spring and Autumn of Chinese Martial Arts—5000 Years*. Santa Cruz: Plum Publishing, 1995. p. 3.
45 "this richly cosmopolitan period": Campbell, *Oriental Mythology*, p. 444.
46 "At a given point the matrix": Kristofer Schipper, *The Taoist Body*. Berkeley: University of California Press, 1993. p. 34.
47 "the results of the studies": Ted Kaptchuk, *The Web That Has No Weaver*. Chicago: Congdon & Weed, 1983. pp. 22–23.
48 "The SupremeUltimate": Zhou Dun-Yi, a translation from Fung Yu-lan's *A Short History of Chinese Philosophy*, p. 269.
49 "The Concept of Yin-Yang": Giovanni Maciocia, *The Foundations of Chinese Medicine: A Comprehensive Text for Acupuncturists and Herbalists*. Edinburgh, London, Melbourne, and New York: Churchill Livingstone, 1993. p. 1.
50 "The theory of Phases": Kaptchuk, *The Web That Has No Weaver*, pp. 343–344.
51 "We have sufficient scientific evidence": Bill Moyers, *Healing and the Mind*. New York: Doubleday, 1993. pp. 180, 182, 186.
52 "Yuan Shen is the body's spiritual element": Jerry Alan Johnson, *Chinese Medical Qigong Therapy: A Comprehensive Clinical Text*. Pacific Grove, Calif.: The International Institute of Medical Qigong, 2000. p. 291. Johnson's book is the first in-depth explanation of medical qigong written for the Western mind. He has pioneered the establishment of medical qigong faculties within American traditional Chinese medicine schools and is a highly regarded martial arts teacher and author.
53 "One follows the breaths up and down": Yin-shun, *The Way to Buddhahood*. Boston: Wisdom Publications, 1998. p. 263.
54 From Huston Smith's *The World's Religions*, p. 85.
55 "All orthodox systems of Indian philosophy": Vivekananda, pp. 269, 788.
56 "Buddhist, unlike the Hindu, systems": Paravahera Vajiranana Mahathera, *Buddhist Meditation*, Introduction.
57 "Nirvana and 'release from the matrix'": *The Book of Balance and Harmony*, translated by Thomas Cleary. San Francisco: North Point Press, 1989. p. 53.

58 "When emptiness is clear": Thomas Cleary, *Vitality, Energy, Spirit*. Boston and London: Shambhala Publications, 1991. pp. 153–154.

59 "All that we are": *Dhammapada*. Bombay: Theosophy Company (India) Private Ltd., 1965. Verse 1.

60 "The continuum begins with interest": Smith, *The World's Religion*, p. 207.

61 "For the Daoist master": Schipper, *Taoist Body*, p. 130.

62 "Yahweh did not remain": Karen Armstrong, *A History of God*, pp. 19–20.

63 "cannot fix its mind's eye": Gregory, taken from Armstrong, *A History of God*, p. 219.

64 "The mystic was engaged": ibid., p. 241.

65 "Teachers, fathers, sons": *Bhagavad Gita*, translated by Annie Besant. Madras: Theosophical Publishing House, 1970. pp. 12, 16, 22, 23.

66 "The doctrine which stands out": Vivekananda, p. 472.

67 "External—stressed the regulation": Draeger and Smith, *Asian Fighting Arts*, p. 17.

68 "The first known grouping": Sun Luang, *Xingyiquan Xue*, translated by Albert Liu, compiled and edited by Dan Miller. Pacific Grove, Calif.: High View Publications, 1993. p. 2.

69 "the whole body should be light": Jou Tsung Hwa, *The Tao of Tai-Chi Chuan*. Rutland: Charles E. Tuttle, 1980. pp. 171–176.

70 "Chan-ssu Chin seeks to unify": ibid., p. 142. Jou's work is one of the most popular English-language books on taijiquan generally. Serious illness pushed Jou to take up taijiquan at the age of forty-seven. His health improved so much that, even in his late seventies, he constantly crisscrossed America teaching taijiquan.

71 "In standing, the body should be erect": ibid., pp. 183–191.

72 "The Bagua is a theory": Master Liang Shou-Yu, Dr. Yang Jwing-Ming, and Mr. Wu Wen-Ching, *Baguazhang (Emei Baguazhang): Theory and Applications*. Jamaica Plain, Mass.: YMAA Publication Center, 1994. p. 22.

73 "specifically work with the body-mind-emotion": Jerry Alan Johnson, *The Essence of Internal Martial Arts, Volume 2*. Pacific Grove, Calif.: Ching Lien Healing Arts Center, 1994. p. 95.

74 "This term, which literally means a 'configuration'": Dukes, *Bodhisattva Warriors*, p. 223.

75 "You begin to understand the theory": Master Liang Shou-Yu and Dr. Yang Jwing-Ming, *Hsing Yi Chuan*. Jamaica Plain, Mass.: YMAA Publication Center, 1990. p. 114.

76 "Knowledge really has no end": Wang Xiangzhai, quoted in Jan Diepersloot, *Warriors of Stillness: The Tao of Yiquan*. Walnut Creek, Calif.: Center for Healing and the Arts, 1999. p. 78.

77 "The standing exercise": ibid., pp. 81–82.

78 "During the Han Dynasty": ibid., pp. 82–83.

79 "modern science only requires one ontological field": Huston Smith, *Forgotten Truth: The Common Vision of the World's Religions*. San Francisco: Harper Collins, 1992. pp. 6, 16. "Weapons, being instruments of ill omen": Cleary, *The Taoist Classics*, pp. 24, 42.

80 "The basic oneness of the universe": Fritjof Capra, *The Tao of Physics*. Boulder: Shambhala Publications, 1983. p. 131.

81 "has led to the impression that some Buddhists": Stephen Batchelor, *The Awakening of the West: The Encounter of Buddhism and Western Culture*. London: Aquarian, 1994. p. 344.

82 "marriage between vipassana-style Indian meditation and Chinese Taoism": Seung Sahn.

83 "They know the world": *Dao De Jing*, from *The Taoist Classic's* translated by Cleary. p. 31.

84 "There is no supernatural": Vivekananda, p. 577.

85 "Neo-Confucianism is indeed the continuations": *A Short History of Chinese Philosophy*, p. 268.

86 "We have contrived": D.T. Suzuki, *Essays in Zen Buddhism, First Series*. London: Rider and Company, 1973. p. 371.

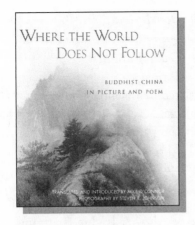

Where the World Does Not Follow:
Buddhist China in Picture and Poem
Translated and introduced
by Mike O'Connor
Photography by Steven R. Johnson
Foreword by William Neill
128 pages, ISBN 0-86171-309-5, $24.95

"The genius of this book is the time-lessness that emerges from juxtaposing modern photographs with T'ang Dynasty Buddhist poetry. The photos or the poetry alone would make this a wonderful text. The two together are something truly special."
—*Shambhala Sun*

"The poetry and photographs, equally captivating, take the reader on a guided tour of China."—*Foreword* magazine

"O'Connor and Johnson provide dual glimpses of Buddhist culture in ancient and modern China. Photographs of the landscape and people of modern China complement the ancient poetry in juxtapositions both surprising and literal. From a row of teacups to misty cliffs to a hermit's retreat, here is a literary and visual tribute to a land where religion and daily life are inseparable."—*Tricycle*

"*Where the World Does Not Follow* is splendid. Not only is it aesthetical-ly beautiful and elegantly laid out but I feel that it fills an important need for most Western Zen practitioners: the photographs, comple-mented by the poems, allow us to experience the world of Joshu and Rinzai as never before. That, surely, can only enhance our grasp of their profound teaching."—Janet Jiryu Abels, Sensei, Still Mind Zendo, New York City

"A beautiful marriage of word and image."—*Publishers Weekly*

Novice to Master:
An Ongoing Lesson in the Extent
of My Own Stupidity
Soko Morinaga
Translated by Belenda Attaway
Yamakawa
Paper: 168 pages, ISBN 0-86171-393-1, $11.95
Cloth: 168 pages, ISBN 0-86171-319-2, $19.95

"Anyone who reads this charming memoir can only wish they had the opportunity to meet this modest yet wise man. It provides rich insight into the protocol of training for the life of a Zen abbot, but is, in many ways, universal—a headstrong young man is forced to conform to a wiser force and shed his arrogance to achieve a higher state of knowledge and serenity. *Novice to Master* serves up the most subtle form of enlightenment."
—*New York Resident*

Chen-Chiu—The Original
Acupuncture:
A New Healing Paradigm
Claus C. Schnorrenberger, M.D.
424 pages, ISBN 0-86171-137-8, $29.95

"Professor Schnorrenberger brings out the full depth of Chinese medical concepts in *Chen-Chiu*. Futhermore, he compares early Chinese and Western philosophical concepts in an exquisite way, pointing out the many ideas both have in common."
—*Journal of the Danish Medical Acupuncture Society*

Mindfulness Yoga: The Awakened Union of Breath, Body, and Mind
Frank Jude Boccio
Foreword by Georg Feuerstein
320 pages, 100 photos,
ISBN 0-86171-335-4, $19.95

"EDITOR'S CHOICE!"—*Yoga Journal*

"Rich with personal stories, and interspersed with guided meditations, *Mindfulness Yoga* offers a way to deeply connect with our bodies and our feelings through yoga. The design of the book is a pleasure. The photos of the poses are clear. Each page stays open so you can practice the pose while referring to the illustration. Both content and design are richly inviting. A must-have for all mindfulness practitioners who also practice or teach yoga."—*The Mindfulness Bell*

Meditation for Life
Martine Batchelor
Photographs by Stephen Batchelor
168 pages, ISBN 0-86171-320-8, $22.95

"Among today's steady stream of new books on Buddhist meditation, most are easy to ignore. This one isn't. It offers simple, concrete instructions in meditation and the photographs are delicious eye candy. Author Martine Batchelor spent 10 years in a Korean monastery and presumably knows a lotus position when she sees one; she also has a sense of humor."—*Psychology Today*

"Graceful, elegant, clear, helpful and wise; *Meditation for Life* demystifies meditation while making it available to all who need it. A treasure."—Mark Epstein, author of *Thoughts without a Thinker*

The Fine Arts of Relaxation,
Concentration, and Meditation:
Ancient Skills for Modern Minds
Joel and Michelle Levey
Foreword by Margaret J. Wheatley
304 pages, ISBN 0-86171-349-4,
$14.95

"Joel and Michelle Levey share more than 100 ideas, practices, and exercises they have used over the past 30 years to teach stress reduction and personal development to companies, groups, and individuals…. Tailor-made for anyone dealing with physical, mental, or emotional stress."
—*Spirituality and Health*

"What a beautiful book! We need so much in our world to focus on how to be instead of how to do, and this book shows the way."
—Larry Dossey, M.D., author of *Space, Time, & Medicine* and *Healing Wounds*

Wisdom Publications

Wisdom Publications, a nonprofit publisher, is dedicated to preserving and transmitting important works from all the major Buddhist traditions as well as works on related East-West themes.

To learn more about Wisdom, or browse our books on-line, visit our website at wisdompubs.org. You may request a copy of our mail-order catalog on-line or by writing to:

Wisdom Publications
199 Elm Street
Somerville, Massachusetts 02144 USA
Telephone: (617) 776-7416
Fax: (617) 776-7841
Email: info@wisdompubs.org
www.wisdompubs.org

Wisdom is a nonprofit, charitable 501(c)(3) organization affiliated with the Foundation for the Preservation of the Mahayana Tradition (FPMT).